D0863536

AWFUL
TRUTHS

THE
AWFUL
TRUTHS

FAMOUS MYTHS, HILARIOUSLY DEBUNKED

by Brian Thomsen

Illustrations by James Fallone

Collins

An Imprint of HarperCollinsPublishers

HarperCollins books may be purchased for educational, business, or sales promotional use. For information please write: Special Markets Department, HarperCollins Publishers, 10 East 53rd Street, New York, NY 10022.

FIRST EDITION

Designed by Emily Cavett Taff

Illustrations by James Fallone

Library of Congress Cataloging-in-Publication Data has been applied for.

ISBN 10: 0-06-083699-7

ISBN 13: 978-0-06-083699-3

06 07 08 09 10 WBC/RRD 10 9 8 7 6 5 4 3 2 1

Dedication

This book is the product of an incomplete education.

It is incomplete because it is still ongoing.

All through my life people have opened my eyes to new and diverse areas, authors, and volumes that have piqued my interest and, as a result, added to my education.

This book is therefore dedicated to those educators of my incomplete education including (but not limited to):

Arthur Thomsen for P.C. Wren; Eileen Thomsen for Arthur Hailey; Donna Thomsen for the New York Yankees and Shakespeare; Homer Lincoln for Alistair Maclean and Robert Heinlein; Isabelle Lincoln for Ray Bradbury and Michael Crichton; Patricia Thomsen for Nancy Drew and Anne Frank; Robert Sabatelli for A. J. P. Taylor; John Connolly for Plato and Michael Oakeshott; Stephen Duffy for Teihlard de Charden; Hildreth Kritzer for Irving Howe and Alfred Kazin; Terry Malley for Leslie Fiedler and Thomas Pynchon; Kathy Malley for Fred L. Worth and Jennifer Wilde; Frank Walsh for Richard Chase and William Faulkner; Diane Otto for Isaac Asimov; Robert Maguire for Robertson Davies; Terri Cullen for Patricia Nell Warren, Taylor Caldwell and Irving Wallace; Bernard Shir-Cliff for Walter Tevis, Andrew Greeley, and Thomas Fleming; David Chesanow for Anthony Burgess; Jo Fletcher for Philip Kerr; Richard Cronin for Jean Paul Sartre; Bill Malloy for Jerome Charyn; Howard Kaminsky for Brooks Stanwood; Tom Doherty for Win Blevins; Bill Fawcett for Dudley Pope; Ken Scott for Francis Parkman, Owen Wister, and

Jack Shaefer; John Kuhl for Stephen King; Marty Miller for John Norman and Norman Mailer; Steffie Miller for Leon Uris; Frank Brady for James Boswell; Allen Kupfer for Rochester, Swinburne, Coleridge, and Roger Corman; William Bloom for Alexander Solzhenitsyn; Mario Sartori for Nathan Aldyne and Ellis Peters; Baird Searles for Alexei Panshin and Thomas Burnett Swann; Susan Allison for Dean Koontz and Robert Holdstock; John Douglas for James Ellroy; Susan C. Stone for Barbara Michaels and Tom Clancy; Robert Sikso for Stuart Kaminsky, William Goldman and Gregory McDonald; John Moran for Dennis Smith and Fredrick Forsyth; Donald Maass for Anne Perry; Tommy Xanthos for Robert Ludlum; Frank Weimann for H. W. Brands and Ron Powers.

As well as Regis High School, Jean Shepherd, Irving Wallace, Winston Churchill, David McCullough, William F. Buckley, Jimmy Breslin, John Gambling, Vin Scelsa, Pete Hamil, Harlan Ellison, Don Imus, Bill Maher, Al Hunt, George Will, Maureen Dowd, E. J. Dionne, Margaret Carlson, James Carville, Robert Novak, Daniel Berrigan, Bob Woodward, Michael Dirda, Otto Penzler, Chris Matthews, Daniel Boorstein, Isaac Asimov, Dale Walker, Sarah Vowell, Martin H. Greenberg, Robert Silverberg, Charlie Rose, Jon Stewart, Brian Lamb . . . and everyone else who inspired me in some way or another to pick up and read a book on a subject that I might not have chosen to if not for their input.

Long may the education continue.

Contents

Introduction

I n the movie *Barbershop* the part that caused the most "water-cooler conversation" was when Cedric the Entertainer maintained three undeniable truths that no one would admit: O.J. was guilty, Rodney King was asking for it, and Rosa Parks was just tired. Whether you agree with him or not on whether those truths are "undeniable," they are most definitely "awful."

Princeton University defines "awful" as the following:

awful
adj 1: exceptionally bad or displeasing; . . . [syn: atrocious, abominable, dreadful, painful, terrible, unspeakable] 2: causing fear or dread or terror; [syn: dire, direful, dread (a), dreaded, dreadful, fearful, fearsome, frightening, horrendous, horrific, terrible] 3: offensive or even (of persons) malicious; . . .

Source: WordNet ® 2.0, © 2003 Princeton University

But just because facts might be "dreadful" or "painful" and events might be "offensive" or "horrific" doesn't make them incorrect.

Facts are composed of truths, and sometimes these truths are indeed awful. Because of their displeasing nature, many of us are inclined to try to forget them—little things like the juvenile criminal record of a favorite actor or actress, or the well-guarded Hollywood secret that a dashing leading man was short, always used a stunt double, or preferred the company of gentlemen . . . or larger matters like moments of shame in our nation's past or lapses of judgment by those we hold in reverence.

But "truths," like facts, are stubborn things, and they just won't go away even if we consciously try to ignore them or avoid them.

They can be inconvenient, distasteful, and displeasing . . . but they're still there.

Consider the following:

- Everyone knows history is written by the victors.

- Everyone knows history is rewritten by those who later assume power.

- Everyone knows history is "more or less bunk," at least according to Henry Ford.

Which is probably why a great many people believe a great many things that are in direct contradiction to readily available facts . . . and a great man by the name of Daniel Patrick Moynihan once said that everybody is entitled to their own opinion, but that doesn't mean that they are entitled to their own facts.

Now, I am not talking about arbitrary matters of allegedly great import that partisans can bicker about on talk radio such as "why we really went into Iraq" or "whether O.J. was framed" or "whether Ben and J Lo will ever find true happiness with or without each other." Those matters still fall into the category of Truth Still Under Construction.

I am talking about incidences, events, people, and projects that are all a matter of public record if anyone feels like indulging in a bit of research.

The subjects range from Hollywood to history and from presidents to pop stars, unveiling little known facts about well-known subjects.

Some facts enlighten.

Some entertain.

Some shock.

And some . . . well, if taken in the full course of human

events, who really cares? (Except the seekers of truth, of course).

For many the facts need to be avoided . . . especially when they don't support one's preconception or one's chosen opinion.

But again facts are stubborn things, and *The Awful Truths* will come out.

All I know is someone called for an exterminator. I suppose
the next thing you're going to tell me is that snakes
aren't naturally found in Ireland…

Saint Patrick wasn't even born in Ireland

He is the most famous Irishman of all time.

What would a March 17 parade be without his image, a Dublin bishop holding betwixt the fingers of one hand a shamrock, and in the other hand a crosier befitting his office, with the remnants of an escaping serpent crushed beneath his sandaled foot?

Saint Patrick is the image of all that is Irish, the seminal Irish Catholic, and the Uncle Sam/John Bull of the Irish nationalist movement that inspired countless rebels to resist Anglo-Protestant domination of the Emerald Isle.

The only problem with this icon:

Saint Patrick was not born in Ireland.

Worse yet, he was English by birth.

This patron saint of Ireland—born 389, died 461—this most famous of all Irishmen (let alone Irish saints) was actually born in Britain, the son of a Roman official named Calpurnius. As the story goes, he was kidnapped by pirates and sold into slavery in County Mayo (Ireland), where he endured the yoke of oppression for six years before finally escaping back to Scotland and entering monastic life. Moving up through the ranks of the British church, he was eventually ordained a missionary bishop to Ireland, where he preached conversion in the northern and western parts of the Emerald Isle.

Much of what we know of him is derived from two works he

authored: *The Confessions* and *Letter to Coroticus*. The stories of his divine dream visitations, his banishment of the snakes, and his use of the shamrock to illustrate the concept of the holy Trinity are unfortunately all apocryphal.

Setting aside the curious fairy tale of how he allegedly cast out all of the snakes from Ireland, the fact that his claim to fame lies in the success of his mission to bring Christianity to Ireland is somewhat ironic, given the role that religion, specifically the schism in Christian sects, has played in the ongoing crucible of pain and oppression that has tortured the Irish for so many years.

Far from being the poster boy of Irish unity, he is rather an icon of that which divides Ireland from its role as an integral part of Great Britain.

He did not foster rebellion nor did he deny his ancestral legacy, and he was every bit as Irish as Lord of the Dance Michael Flatley and the legendary Irish tenor Dennis Day (neither of whom were born on the Emerald Isle).

'Tis a shame that the Irish elevated one of the interlopers as their patron saint.

Surely someone homegrown from the Irish sod would have been a better choice to lead the parade and buy the first round on St. Patty's Day.

"A Nation Once Again" . . . er . . . for the first time

One of the most popular Irish "rebel songs" is titled "A Nation Once Again."

Indeed, it is hard to walk through an Irish American neighborhood on St. Patty's Day without hearing its memorable chorus slurred by the revelers with all of their hearts.

When boyhood's fire was in my blood
I read of ancient freemen,
Of Greece and Rome who bravely stood,
Three hundred men and three men;
And then I prayed I yet might see
Our fetters rent in twain,
And Ireland, long a province, be
A nation once again!

A nation once again,
A nation once again,
And Ireland, long a province, be
A nation once again!

So from the time, through wildest woe,
That hope has shone a far light,
Nor could love's brightest summer glow
Outshine that solemn starlight,
It seemed to watch above my head

In forum, field and fame,
Its angel voice sang round my bed,
A nation once again.

A nation once again,
A nation once again,
And Ireland, long a province, be
A nation once again!

It whisper'd too, that freedom's ark,
And service high and holy,
Would be profaned by feeling dark
And passions vain or lowly;
For, freedom comes from God's right hand,
And needs a godly train;
And righteous men must make our land
A nation once again!

A nation once again,
A nation once again,
And Ireland, long a province, be
A nation once again!

So, as I grew from boy to man
I bent me to that bidding
The spirit of each selfish plan
And cruel passions ridding
For, thus I hoped some day to aid
Oh, can such hope be vain
When my dear country shall be made
A nation once again.

A nation once again,
A nation once again,
And Ireland long a province, be
A nation once again!

The song was written way back in the 1840s by Thomas Osbourne Davis, an Irish Catholic leader working toward the independence of Ireland from the English forces that occupied the Emerald Isle.

There's just one problem.

The title is a misnomer.

In order for the title to be accurate, Ireland would have had to have been a nation once before and at some point stopped being a nation.

Neither is actually true.

A nation is defined as "a politically organized body of people under a single government" or "a people who share common customs, origins, history, and frequently language."

Contrary to popular propaganda, Ireland has never existed as the former. Even in the days of the High King, the Emerald Isle was riddled with warring factions and tribal sectionalism even under the iron rule of such notables as Brian Boru and Sigurd the Stout . . . and, needless to say, these tribal differences (including customs and languages/dialects) fairly well exclude the latter condition as well.

Once Henry II of England gained control of Ireland in 1172, there was a continued alien ruling presence on the isle even if its dominion at times only included "the Pale," which is now the area around Dublin. The Act of Union with England in 1801, though it parliamentarily established British dominion over the isle, never succeeded in uniting *all* of Ireland under a single recognized government. Indeed, it might be more accurate to say that Ireland was part of the English nation at this point.

As a result, it is safe to say that Ireland has never been its own nation, and the only proper answer to the plea "a nation once again" would be the return of all of Ireland to British rule, an outcome that would be anathema to all goodly singers of rebel songs.

In a 2002 BBC World Services poll of listeners, "A Nation Once Again" was voted the most popular tune, beating out the best of the Beatles, the Rolling Stones, Willie Nelson, and the Spice Girls.

But as this book went to press, the title was still a misnomer.

Shakespeare—great playwright, lousy historian

F ew would ever debate that William Shakespeare is the greatest playwright of all time. The identity of the author, whether he was in reality Francis Bacon or Thomas Kyd or perhaps a consortium of paid playwrights working together, or simply a fellow named Will, a glover's son who set forth from Stratford-upon-Avon to ply the trade of the dramatist in London, is really inconsequential.

The quality of works speaks for itself, and indeed what a canon of work it is. The classic drama of young lovers in *The Tragedy of Romeo and Juliet*, the archetypal lover driven insane by jealousy in *The Tragedy of Othello, the Moor of Venice*, the manipulative and ambitious wife Lady Macbeth, and the conniving and legalistic Shylock in *The Merchant of Venice* are a mere handful of his most memorable characters.

The eloquence of his prose is exemplified in soliloquies that begin with such lines as "To be or not to be: that is the question," "the quality of mercy is not strain'd, it droppeth as the gentle rain from heaven," "All the world's a stage," and, of course, "Friends, Romans, countrymen; lend me your ears." It is equaled only by his own proficiency in poetry, including the famed sonnets such as "Shall I compare thee to a summer's day" and "My mistress' eyes are nothing like the sun."

There is no doubt about it. When it comes to English literature, Shakespeare was the *man*!

But the awful truth is the bard was also a pretty lousy historian, which might not be as much of a factor if he hadn't labeled many of his plays as histories.

There have been numerous apologists for his mistakes and manipulations. Indeed, Restoration poet/playwright/critic John Dryden, who coined the term "poetic/dramatic license," set the stage for the acceptance of the chronicles of history as a malleable backdrop for creative works of art. The play is the thing, and sometimes events have to be manipulated for dramatic effect.

With Shakespeare, however, the frequency and types of errors that are recurrent in his work suggest slightly different motives—either he didn't know or he didn't care, and in either case one would have to conclude that either disposition would be enough to label one a lousy historian.

First, there are the small details whose anachronistic nature stand out. There are numerous references, for example, to clocks and the telling of time in the play *The Tragedy of Julius Caesar*, which is exceptionally problematic since the clock had not yet been invented in 44 B.C., the year in which the historical events depicted in the play actually took place. Likewise in act one of *The Life and Death of King John*, the king threatens to use cannon against his enemy, despite the fact that they had not yet been introduced into use for warfare in Britain at that time. Such throwaway details clearly indicate a degree of carelessness on matters of historical accuracy because their necessary relevance to the larger work is questionable at best.

In simple terms, the anachronisms are thematically unnecessary and should have been corrected.

Second, the bard changes historic details in his characterizations of actual personages, thus rendering them inaccurate. A perfect example of this is the character of Prince Hal, who, over the course of several plays, eventually becomes Henry V. Not only is he presented as a contemporary of his rival Hotspur (who was actually close to twenty years older than him), he is also portrayed as being monolingual, and unable to converse in French. In reality he would have learned the language while still a youth by simply conversing with his own relatives. What's more, in the same play his future bride is equally ignorant of English, despite the fact that it would have been a normal part of her education in the French court.

Third, there are numerous omissions of major events in the bard's historical plays where five turbulent years (such as the five between Agincourt in 1415 and the Treaty of Troyes in 1420 in the Henry plays) pass with nary a mention and the simple change of a scene. Other overlooked events include the signing of the Magna Carta (1215) in *The Life of Death of King John*, the Peasants' Revolt (1381) in *The Tragedy of King Richard II*, and the numerous contributions to arts and sciences made by the eponymous monarch in *The Famous History of the Life of Henry VIII* that would have rounded out the character of the king in terms of character depth and not just physical girth of figure (not to mention the byplay with such real characters as Cromwell and Thomas More, who provided historical fodder for Robert Bolt in *A Man for All Seasons*). At least a passing reference is warranted when one claims one's play to be "The famous history of . . ."

True, a dramatist can sometimes take liberties for dramatic or thematic effect as the bard does so eloquently in *The Life of Henry V* in his depiction of the Battle of Agincourt. Historians generally agree that it was the English advantage with the longbow that assured their victory over the French. Yet the bows and arrows of outrageous bowmen are largely unseen and relegated to the offstage background so that the bard can concentrate on Henry's fighting man to man alongside the troops in the field. Shakespeare uses this "band of brothers" scene to help flesh out the image of Henry as a heroic military leader. He doesn't deny the presence of the longbow as a determining factor. Bowmen are indeed mentioned—they are just not active players on the stage alongside the king.

The bard's works' inadequacy as history does not diminish their value as literature. Indeed, Shakespeare lived in a time when even recent history was subject to revision, depending on who was on the throne at the given time. Certainly more than a few others who earned their living with a quill were said to have lost their heads under Elizabeth for not promulgating the preferred account of the lives of various personages in her noble lineage.

I don't care what the Greeks had or didn't have.
If I don't have a car chase and a rap singer as the star,
Troilus and Cressida isn't gonna pull the sixteen- to
twenty-four-year-olds…

Nathan Hale—terrorist of the attack on New York, 9/21

There is perhaps no more romanticized a name from the American Revolution than that of Nathan Hale.

Hale, a young schoolteacher hanged as a spy for the American cause on September 22, 1776, has become the archetypal martyr-hero of the Revolution, representing patriotism, courage, and loyalty.

His chilling words from the gallows—"I regret that I have but one life to give for my country"—set the standard for all who aspire to the role of patriot.

But the awful truth of the matter is that most of this story is no closer to historic fact than the early reports from the Pentagon regarding Jessica Lynch or Pat Tillman (whose meritorious service, heroism, and bravery are in no way diminished by the fallacious spin that was released to the media).

Fact: Nathan Hale was hanged on September 22, 1776, in New York City.

Fact: He was working under the command of forces led by George Washington.

Everything else, well, dubious.

His chilling last words?

Hale probably paraphrased Joseph Addison, the playwright, with something along the lines of "If I had a thousand lives I would lay them all down, if called to do so in defense of my injured bleeding country" (or some such statement, as actual accounts of the incident conflict). Addison's actual words were: "How beautiful is death, when earn'd by virtue!/Who would not be that youth? What pity is it/That we can die but once to serve our country!" Hale's version: very derivative, much less eloquent.

A young schoolteacher?

Hale was an enlistee in the Continental Army. True he had taught school upon his graduation from Yale, but that stopped being his profession once he entered the military. The fact that he was using his Yale degree as a cover is incidental; he was passing himself off to the British as a Dutch teacher, which is not the same thing as being someone who teaches Dutch.

In actuality, what he was really doing was being a spy, and not a particularly good one at that, while also engaging in acts of terrorism.

Hale's instincts as a spy were questionable at best. One must look only to his five months on garrison duty in and around New York. During such time there are accounts that he regularly played ball on the Bowery in full view of many of the British-sympathizing folks whom he was now trying to infiltrate (New York having changed hands and under British rule in the time that passed since he had left garrison duty). Many had seen him in uniform (one of the reasons why soldiers were clearly discouraged from volunteering for spy duty—their identities and allegiances were already a matter of public record). A further bit of evidence that his "spying" was inadequate—his first assignment wound up being his last.

As to his engaging in acts of terrorism?

Noted bestselling author and historian Thomas Fleming has put forth a compelling argument that Hale was really executed for having taken part in an act of terrorism, noting that two of the accounts of his arrest clearly notate that he was arrested "with matches in his pocket," which might explain why he wasn't tried as a spy (a formality, but one that was usually practiced), and why his body was left for several days as a warning to others. Why? Spies knew that if they were caught and convicted, they would be executed. Insurgents and terrorists, however, were another story. Civilian upstarts were always causing trouble . . . even in peacetime . . . and, therefore, could not necessarily be tied to aiding and abetting the enemy. Hale's actions, however, were not determined to be just the work of some careless roustabout whose tirade got out of hand. All of this ties in with what had occurred in New York on the previous day, and why the presence of matches in Hale's pocket may have been the evidence that assured his execution.

Though the line "and, of course, if you or any of your IMF team are caught or killed in the course of your mission, the secretary [or president] will disavow any knowledge of the matter" may have originated with the 1960s TV series *Mission: Impossible,* this pragmatic practice at the highest levels of the government has been pro forma for years (e.g., Ike's denial of the famed cold war U-2 incident until Francis Gary Powers's presence in Soviet custody exposed the facts).

Washington, for whom Hale was either serving as a spy or as a junior officer, had a quandary. All of his military advisers agreed that New York City had strategic value to whoever held it, and that, since many New Yorkers were inclined toward being sympathetic toward the Tories (if not actual Tories themselves), and more concerned with the day-to-day operations of their businesses rather than the long-term goals of the War for Independence, a British-occupied New York would be no different for most New Yorkers than one under Washington's control . . . with the significant difference that it would be the British that was now in control of its strategic value.

As a result, Washington and his leading military advisers were of a single mind: If New York were to fall into enemy hands, it should be destroyed, thus depriving the English forces under General William Howe of its value.

Washington's problem, though, was that none of his civilian superiors had agreed to this course of action, and indeed he had been specifically ordered not to engage in such an operation.

Yet preparations were certainly in the works, and, according to Fleming,

> For three previous days small squads of New Englanders, mostly from Connecticut (from which Nathan hailed), had infiltrated the city disguised as farmers eager to sell their

produce. At the bottom of carts loaded with corn were dozens of logs dipped in rosin. A touch of a match and they would create a stupendous blaze. Supplies of similar "combustibles," as they were called, may have been left at strategic points.

And on the day before Hale was captured and executed, "shortly after midnight on Saturday, September 21," a cry that every eighteenth-century city dweller dreaded was heard in New York's streets: "FIRE!" The wind was blowing briskly from the South, and the flames, which broke out first in a wooden house near Whitehall ferry slip, swept north with a rapidity that stunned the British. Admiral Lord Richard Howe ordered ashore hundreds of sailors from the fleet to fight the blaze, and two regiments of the army's 3rd Brigade, stationed just north of the city, rushed to help. As they went to work, flames exploded in five or six other places far away from Whitehall. Moreover, the sailors and soldiers found that most fire engines had been sabotaged, hoses cut, and even handles amputated from the fire buckets. . . . Within two hours a huge conflagration was raging. "The wind was so strong," one British officer wrote, "that it was almost impossible to face it, for smoke and flakes of fire." General Howe refused to commit his whole army to fighting the blaze, fearing it might be part of a plan to attack his forward positions. At daybreak the fire was still burning out of control, having cut a huge swath from Whitehall up the west side of the city. Captain Frederick MacKenzie of the Royal Welsh fusiliers, who reached the city around this time, wrote in his diary that it was "almost impossible to conceive a scene of more horror and distress. . . . The sick, the aged, women and children half naked were seen going they knew not where, taking refuge in houses which were at a distance from the fire, but from whence they were in several instances driven a second and even a third time" (from the *New York* magazine article "The True Story of Nathan ['The Torch'] Hale: No Wonder They Hanged Him" by Thomas Fleming).

Close to a thousand buildings, most possessing little military value, totaling literally a quarter of the city, were destroyed to deprive the British of its "strategic value" and to send a message to the city's Tory sympathizers.

According to one account of his interrogation, Hale basically admitted to following orders from his commander in chief, but did not further elaborate. Fleming notes that Hale had volunteered to be a spy, he was not ordered to be such, ergo, his "orders" must have referred to something else, perhaps something that might account for the matches he had in his possession.

Washington never admitted to authorizing such a mission: he was on record as having been ordered *not* to authorize such a mission.

When asked about how it might have occurred, he once conjectured, "[perhaps by] Providence or some good honest fellow [who] has done more for us than we were disposed to do for ourselves," a judgment probably not shared by the innocent civilian victims of this terrorist act, performed in the name of the War for Independence.

At least three U.S. presidents had to be bailed out financially after leaving office

You didn't always have to be wealthy in order to have a shot at being president, though personal family fortunes never hurt.

You also didn't always have an expectation of financial independence after your presidency was over.

The presidency, simply put, was government service.

It did provide a good living with a cap for government salaries that assured its eminence (i.e., no one was allowed to earn a governmental salary whose base pay exceeded that of the president's).

By no means was it a surefire method to amass a family fortune either, although during your term of office you and your family lived room and board free, as well as enjoyed numerous other conveniences and niceties in terms of transportation and entertainment.

What it did do in most cases was to increase your expectation in terms of your continued standard of living after your term of office expired. In most cases, such a lifestyle would be very expensive to maintain . . . particularly when one was unemployed after a noticeable absence from the private sector and a gap in the marketable skills such years usually produced to keep one in sync with the job market.

Before there were his-and-her seven-figure book contracts for the retiring and/or deposed president and first lady, or contracts for TV punditry, or whirlwind corporate lecture tours that pay the speakers per minute a rate rivaling that of your average NFL player, the leaders of the United States of America often needed to concern themselves with not just managing the country but also the family business as well.

In numerous cases their management of the family business was less than exemplary.

Even the best of presidents sometimes found themselves in the red.

George Washington's greatest claim to possessing a keen acumen for finance and business rests solely on his decision to marry a rich widow in order to separate himself from a domineering mother. (His mother was the primary reason he excelled in the military, as he often volunteered for missions that would keep him from returning to the family farm and back under her thumb.)

Indeed, once the war was over, Washington openly expressed his desire to return to his wife and get the family back in order, but when the Continental Congress knocked, they, borrowing the parlance of Mario Puzo for a moment, made him an offer he couldn't refuse.

He was their choice to be the first president of the United States, an offer he freely accepted.

One of the benefits of the job as defined by the Congress was a princely annual salary of $25,000, which George quickly declined in the name of the honor and integrity of the office and in deference to the huge debts the newborn country had rung up in its War of Independence.

Unfortunately, this first president didn't really think through what he was doing.

By declining his salary, Washington found himself and the family farm going broke as his attentions were obviously diverted to matters of state. Several of the changes he intended to make to get the farm back on a profitable track after it had been managerially neglected during the war were never properly introduced. As a result, he, the president, wound up having to petition Congress for a series of loans to keep his family business out of bankruptcy. This resulted in a slight shift in the balance of power away from the executive branch since he who controls the purse strings pays the fiddler, and he who pays the fiddler calls the dance.

* * *

James Madison left the executive branch to return to his farm in Virginia, fully expecting to live out the rest of his years in retirement off the estate that he had amassed to date. Unfortunately, several seasons of less-than-stellar crops and more than sizable gambling debts led him to once again seek out public service in the name of a salary. He subsequently accepted a position as a rector of the University of Virginia and another at the 1829 Constitutional Convention representing Orange County, Virginia. After Madison's death, his wife, the well-loved Dolley, had to sell his private papers to Congress and to sell the family home at Montpelier to take care of all of the family debts.

Prior to his presidency, Ulysses S. Grant achieved a level of success during the Civil War that far surpassed anything he had done in civilian life, and indeed his war-hero status probably had a great deal to do with his election to the highest office in the land. After serving two terms he retired to New York and invested his entire savings in a business venture with his son, through his firm Grant & Ward. But corruption, mismanagement, and embezzlement on the behalf of his son's partner quickly decimated Grant's fortune, leaving the family on the verge of insolvency.

This situation led Grant to start a new presidential tradition—financing one's postpresidency life through the sale of one's memoirs. (Note: This is a clever evolution of the solution arrived at by Dolley Madison, with the exception that the papers were purchased by a noncongressional entity for eventual publication.)

He finished the book on his deathbed, and it became a huge bestseller, leaving his family debt free and refinanced.

Harry S Truman ran into similar straits after his presidency. Truman was known as a failed haberdasher prior to his career in politics, and he worked his way up through the governmental ranks as a cog in the Tom Prendergast political machine. Prior to his ascension at the death of Franklin Delano Roosevelt, he was a party man through and through. Yet, despite his prior party loyalty, few choices were made available to him by the party upon his retirement. In 1953, corporations began offering him positions to serve on their boards of directors for extremely generous compensation, complete with numerous fringe benefits. Truman, however, rejected every offer, saying, "You don't want me. You want the office of the president, and that doesn't belong to me. It belongs to the American people, and it is not for sale."

Indeed, Truman and his wife, Bess, after having taken part in the inauguration of Dwight D. Eisenhower, quietly boarded a train bound for Missouri without honor guard or fanfare, trusting that the good folks back home would provide for them. His retirement was subsequntly subsidized by a hefty, far beyond fair market value, book advance for his memoirs, which soon shocked the New York publishing community by eventually earning out.

Truman's health began to fail in the mid-sixties, and then president Lyndon B. Johnson issued an executive order that made military medical personnel available to former presidents at their home. The fact that Johnson was just months away from his own retirement at the time may have influenced his decision to assist his predecessor.

Nowadays, the seven-figure book advance is status quo for ex-presidents (though it should be noted that prior to Bill Clinton's *My Life*, the published works of first ladies almost always outsold those of their executive husbands, even when the books were coauthored by a family pet), as are corporately subsidized housing, luxurious lecture tours, and other benefits of the jet set.

Coupled with the presidential pension, even life after the White House can be pretty sweet when compared to the lifestyles of the majority of people who did the electing (members of the Supreme Court notwithstanding).

Thomas Jefferson, active slave owner

Anyone who has ever seen any of the dramatic presentations of the birth of the United States has to be impressed by the quasi-egalitarian stance of tall, young Thomas Jefferson. His change of the simple words "life, liberty, and property" to "life, liberty, and the pursuit of happiness" is said to have set the course for a truly democratic America. Jefferson's further Continental Congress skirmishes on the condemnation of slavery and the issue of whether such views should be included in our foundational documents is also easily apparent (such as in his arguments over the Declaration of Independence, where he wanted to include a reference charging that the crown "has waged cruel war against human nature itself, violating its most sacred rights of life and liberty in the persons of a distant people who never offended him, captivating & carrying them into slavery in another hemisphere . . .").

Indeed one need go no further than his own private writings to reveal the evidence of his own personal disdain for slavery:

There must doubtless be an unhappy influence on the manners of our people produced by the existence of slavery among us. The whole commerce between master and slave is a perpetual exercise of the most boisterous passions, the most unremitting despotism on the one part, and degrading submissions on the other. Our children see this, and learn to imitate it; for man is an imitative animal. . . . Indeed I tremble for my country when I reflect that God is just: that his justice cannot sleep for ever: that considering numbers, nature and natural means only, a revolution of the wheel of fortune, an exchange of situation, is among possible events: that it may become probable by supernatural interference! The Almighty has no attribute which can take side with us in such a context. But it is impossible to be temperate and to pursue this subject through the various considerations of policy, of morals, of history natural and civil. We must be contented to hope they will force their way into every one's mind. I think a change already perceptible, since the origin of the present revolution. The spirit of the master is abating, that of the slave rising from the dust, his condition mollifying, the way I hope preparing, under the auspices of heaven, for a total emancipation, and that this is disposed, in the order of events, to be with the consent of the masters, rather than by their extirpation.

His private correspondence also shows evidence of his personal antipathy toward slavery:

To: Mr. Benjamin Banneker
     Philadelphia, August 30, 1791

Sir,

I thank you, sincerely, for your letter of the 19th instant, and for the Almanac it contained. No body wishes more than I do, to see such proofs as you exhibit, that nature has given to our black brethren talents equal to those of the other colors of men; and that the appearance of the want of them, is owing merely to the degraded condition of their existence, both in Africa and America. I can add with truth, that no body wishes more ardently to see a good system commenced, for raising the condition, both of their body and mind, to what it ought to be, as far as the imbecility of their present existence, and other circumstances, which cannot be neglected, will admit.

I have taken the liberty of sending your Almanac to Monsieur de Condozett, Secretary of the Academy of Sciences at Paris, and Member of the Philanthropic Society, because I considered it as a document, to which your whole color had a right for their justification, against the doubts which have been entertained of them.

I am with great esteem, Sir, Your most obedient Humble Servant,

Thomas Jefferson

There is very little room for doubt that Thomas Jefferson abhorred slavery . . . but the awful truth of the matter is that he was also an active slave owner and actually opposed the emancipation of slaves in the United States. He believed that if people of the United States (read, the entire country, not just an enlightened few) ever decided to abolish slavery, the only sensible solution would be to repatriate them back to the islands or Africa, or perhaps set up an independent colony for them.

Under no circumstances did he ever see them as just blending in to American society.

At the Jefferson Memorial in Washington, D.C., there is an inscription from his autobiography that reads: "Nothing is more certainly written in the book of fate, than that these people are to be free." Intentionally omitted is the rest of the quote, which reads: "nor is it less certain that the two races, equally free, cannot live in the same government. Nature, habit, opinion have drawn indelible lines of distinction between them."

Indeed, when the great Polish patriot Thaddeus Kościuszko (who fought in the American Revolutionary War under George Washington and was awarded by the U.S. Congress the rank of brigadier general) entrusted Jefferson to carry out his posthumous directive to emancipate all of his slaves, the former president refused, fearing an anarchistic outcome that would adversely affect both the slaves and those around them.

As to Jefferson's own business/personal dealings with his own slaves, it is true that his personal records do reveal that he owned as many as 187 field slaves at one time. Most of these, however, he inherited from his wife's father, along with various other pieces of property. His "independent ownership" of them is further complicated because they functioned as part of the collateral he used for various debts, thus inhibiting him from simply setting them free, even if that were his own personal view and intent.

Jefferson went so far as to lobby for the curtailment of the importation of slaves, but he always seemed to stop short of calling for its enforced abolition.

Needless to say, the third president was obviously torn on this issue.

So then what about that master/slave thing he had with Sally Hemings?

This is another issue that is far from simple.

It's complicated.

Complicated in the way that most family matters are.

Though Jefferson was indeed a slave owner, he was far from the lascivious Simon Legree of Down South plantation stereotypes.

He did not purchase her to be his mistress, nor is there any evidence that he ever forced himself upon her.

For all of the notorious scandals and headlines about Jefferson having a slave as a mistress, a more accurate and possibly even more scandalous headline might read: JEFFERSON TAKES WIFE'S HALF SISTER AS MISTRESS.

. . . because after an acceptable period of mourning over his wife's death, that is exactly what he did. In addition to being a part of the property that he had inherited from his wife's father's estate, Sally Hemings was also the illegitimate daughter of John Wayles, his father-in-law.

As the story goes, Jefferson first became acquainted with Sally when she accompanied his daughter on her trip to Paris while he was stationed there performing his diplomatic duties. She had been a housemaid back at Monticello, exempt from fieldwork and domination by the overseer, and had attended his wife's bedside during her final days. She no doubt, therefore, must have overheard his promise to his beloved spouse that he would never remarry. In addition to Sally's resemblance to his deceased and well-loved wife, the color-blind egalitarianism of France in transition helped to foster the relationship that allegedly led to the conception of their first child together during this trip.

Despite the fact that under French law Sally could have remained in France a free woman, she returned with Jefferson to Monticello, where they maintained a discreet but evidently loving relationship for the rest of his years.

Thus, rather than being the female slave bent to her master's will, she was indeed his willing consort.

Further evidence of their love lies in Jefferson's own will.

Having made his opinions on emancipation known via the aforementioned Kościuszko matter, it is quite notable that his will specificaly included the emancipation of all of Sally's (and, ergo, probably his) children.

Indeed, these were the only slaves he emancipated.

Even strongly held personal views are allowed to be altered in matters concerning family.

The Alamo was not necessarily a heroic last stand

E ven before the Texas War for Independence had been completed, the siege at the Alamo had already achieved mythic status.

The final assault on the former mission stronghold came before daybreak on the morning of March 6, 1836. Columns of Mexican soldiers emerged from the predawn darkness and headed for the walls. Cannon fire and small-arms shots from the remaining members of the garrison greeted them. The Texan force inside the Alamo beat back several attacks. But the Mexicans, who greatly outnumbered the cornered opposition, eventually scaled the walls and rushed into the compound. Once inside, they turned captured cannon on the long barrack and church, blasting open the barricaded doors. The defenders were overwhelmed. By sunrise, the battle had ended, and General Antonio López de Santa Anna entered the Alamo compound to survey the scene of his victory and slaughter any and all survivors.

The clarion call of "Remember the Alamo" led Sam Houston's forces to victory at the Battle of San Jacinto a month and a half later, and the names William Travis, James Bowie, and Davy Crockett entered the pantheon of great American warriors.

But this most memorable last stand in the annals of American history may not have been as heroic or even as significant as most folks might wish to believe.

To begin with, this great and noble force for the Texas quest for independence was engaging in their last stand in direct contradiction to the orders of their leader, Sam Houston, who had previously dispatched a message to abandon the mission and blow up any munitions that had to be left behind.

Like Chinese Gordon at Khartoum later in the century, these men died defending a fortification that had already been written off by the nominal powers that be.

Santa Anna had also dispatched numerous messages to those inside the mission walls that if anyone laid down their arms, they would be free to pass through his lines and avoid the consequences of the final siege. Moreover, the Mexican leader's forces were spread out in such a manner as to allow unsullied escape from the Texan encampment without notice or harm.

The further allegation that the men inside the Alamo were holding out to buy time for Sam Houston either to come to the rescue or to amass a larger Texan army is also completely ludicrous and unfounded, based on the records of what Houston was actually doing at the time. As far he knew, the Alamo was already past business, a matter dealt with, the prospects for victory already abandoned . . . or, more colloquially, it was "spilt milk" and was no longer worthy of his attention.

Finally, there is the myth that it was a total massacre with nary a survivor . . . and perhaps by nineteenth-century Texas standards that might have been true since all of the Texas volunteers who had taken up arms were killed. This number, however, did not include everyone who was defending the Alamo. As it turned out, more than twenty women and children who withstood the entire period of siege were spared, as were several male slaves (including William Travis's own African American manservant Joe). Since women, children, and slaves didn't vote in the new Texas, their survival was probably considered to be insignificant.

Thus, the awful truth of the matter is that the men of the Alamo acted against orders from their high command, failed to take advantage of opportunities to live and fight another day for the glory of Texas, and basically engaged in a suicidal last stand for no practical, pragmatic, or strategic gain whatsoever.

Such is called heroism deep in the heart of Texas in the nineteenth century.

Hold fast! If we stick together, we can
hold them off, right Davy…Davy?

But Davy Crockett was still a hero and one of the last men standing there, right?

Well, that depends.
According to a semicontemporary (1837) song:

To the memory of Crockett fill up your to the brim!
The hunter, the hero, the bold yankee yeoman!
Let the flowing oblation be poured forth to him
Who ne'er turned his back on his friend or his foeman
And grateful shall be
His fame to the free;
Fill! fill! to the brave for Liberty bled—
May his name and his fame to the last—Go ahead!

When the Mexicans leaguered thy walls, Alamo!
Twas Crockett looked down on the war-storm's commotion,
And smiled, as by thousands the foe spread below,
And rolled o'er the plain, like the waves of the ocean.
The Texans stood there—
Their flag fanned the air,
And their shout bade the foe try what freeman will dare
What receked they, tho' thousands the prairies o'erspread?
The word of their leader was still—Go ahead!

They came! Like the sea-cliff that laughs at the flood,
Stood that dread band of heroes the onslaught repelling;
Again! And again! Yet undaunted they stood;

While Crocket's deep voice o'er the wild din was swelling.
"Go ahead" was his cry,
"Let us conquer or die;
"And shame to the wretch and the dastard who'd fly!"
And still, mid the battle-cloud, lurid and red,
Rang the hero's dread cry—Go ahead! Go ahead!

He fought—but no valour that horder could withstand;
He fell—but behold where the wan victor found him!
With a smile on his lip, and his rifle in hand,
He lay, with his foeman heaped redly around him;
His heart poured its tide
In the cause of its pride,
A freeman he lived, and a freeman he died;
For liberty struggled, for liberty bled—
May his name and his fame to the last—Go ahead!

(Walt Disney latched onto this motif with his Fess Parker–starring Davy Crockett series having Davy and Georgie Russell singing "Be sure you're right—then go ahead!" throughout the five episodes that were produced for *The Wonderful World of Color* television series.)

A heroic incident worthy of song, a great moment in Americana, . . . but for Davy Crockett it was just another incident in a life lived large.

How do we know it was a "life lived large"?

Because he told us so himself.

During his lifetime (and for at least the ten years following), there were numerous autobiographical accounts of his exploits "written by himself" (at least according to their titles), one of which even covered his exploits in Texas. Numerous anecdotes about his rapport with wild animals; his frontier acumen, bravery, honesty; and his all-around "well-loved-ness by one and all" seem to be more akin to a public relations campaign than an actual historical record, casting him as the second coming of Daniel Boone and the successor to Andrew Jackson on the road to the White House.

The awful truths of his life are slightly less impressive.

He was born in Tennessee in 1786, the fifth of eight children.

He received little in the way of formal education.

In 1813 he enlisted in the Second Regiment of Tennessee Volunteer Mounted Riflemen for ninety days, serving under General (later, President) Andrew Jackson in the campaign against the Creek Indians.

From this point on, Crockett merged short-term military assignments (usually as a scout or militiaman) with local politics, until 1821, when he got elected to the Tennessee legislature. He eventually parlayed his legislator's seat into a successful run for Congress in 1826 and 1828, largely based on his popularity and legacy of tall-tale exploits that had already begun to pervade the pop culture of the time.

He lost reelection in 1830 but regained his seat in 1832.

One of "the narratives of his life by himself" appeared in 1834 and sold like hotcakes, which probably partially assuaged him when he once again lost reelection.

In 1835 he ran again and lost again. His concession speech, it is alleged, included the line "You may all go to hell, and I will go to Texas," which he did, eventually winding up at the Alamo.

He was married twice and had seven legitimate children of record.

His congressional record was largely undistinguished, though he did oppose his own party and the president in regard to the Indian Removal Act.

What he did manage to do was fit into a hero-hungry niche of the evolving American collective mind that had latched onto the hagiographies of Parson Weems (such as his books on George Washington and Francis Marion) in search of "real" American heroes.

As to his part at the Alamo, recent studies are basically split into two camps:

The first one acknowledged that he was definitely there (as evidenced by a reference in one of Colonel William Barrett Travis's letters that Davy was seen encouraging those on guard duty on the walls of the Alamo), but he probably didn't survive to the day of the final siege.

The other camp's beliefs are slightly more bizarre.

According to the papers of José Enrique de la Peña, who served with Santa Anna, Davy survived the siege and was taken before Santa Anna himself, who ordered his summary execution.

This account would obviously play up the larger-than-life aspects of Davy Crockett, legendary hero, and one of the last men standing at the Alamo, if it weren't for the fact that de la Peña claims that Crockett made the following statement in his own defense:

> I am David Crockett, a citizen of the state of Tennessee and representative of a district of that State in the United States Congress. I have come to Texas on a visit of exploration; purposing, if permitted, to become a loyal citizen of the Republic of Mexico. I extended my visit to San Antonio and called in the Alamo to become acquainted with the officers, and learn of them what I could of the condition of affairs. Soon after my arrival, the fort was invested by government troops, whereby I have been prevented from leaving it. And here I am yet, a noncombatant and foreigner, having taken no part in the fighting.

(Or in very loose translation: "There has been a terrible mistake. I wasn't with those guys. I belong with you guys. Surely we can work this out. I really want to be a Mexican, which should make you feel honored since I am, er, was a member of Congress. So please let me go!")

Not exactly the most heroic last words, if you ask me.

It should be noted the de la Peña papers need to be taken with a grain of salt; they have received a great deal of scrutiny and are considered to be of dubious validity by many in recent years.

Then again, I guess the same could be said of the entire heroic canon of the legend of Davy Crockett, no matter what Walt Disney or John Wayne or Ron Howard might have told you via their silver-screen renditions of his days at the Alamo.

The Awful Truth

is
That These
Famous Masterworks

The Wasteland *by T. S. Eliot*

The Great Gatsby *by F. Scott Fitzgerald*

&

Stranger in a Strange Land *by Robert Heinlein*

Were Originally Titled

He Do the Police in Different Voices

Trimalchio in West Egg

&

The Man from Mars

Lee was not first in his class, and Grant was not last

There is an academic proclivity to compare and contrast great military leaders of opposing sides.

One of Stephen Ambrose's earliest works was on General George Armstrong Custer and Indian warrior chief Crazy Horse. Dennis Showalter recently did an exceptional volume entitled *Patton and Rommel*, and numerous Civil War scholars have assayed compare-and-contrast volumes on the great generals of the North and South in the War Between the States, namely Ulysses S. Grant and Robert E. Lee.

Though much of this scholarship is exemplary, many simplistic myths have entered the popular mythos on the Civil War. Most of these, however, are based on several facile judgments and inaccurate facts, many of which have been distorted to support the accuracy of the myths.

There is one school of thought that likes to cast Grant's victory over Lee as pragmatic experience over academic scholarship, or, more simply, bad student grunt Grant over top scholar ivory tower Lee.

Head of the class versus dead last.

This and other such myths deserve to be debunked on multiple levels.

True, at the time of the firing on Fort Sumter and the beginning of the war, Grant was working in the family leather business, having already failed in such areas as real estate, farming, custom house work, and the military itself (having resigned a captaincy after being reprimanded for drinking), while Lee had finished a stint as superintendent of West Point, a position worthy of its "ivory tower" label, and had retained his commission in the military up to the day he resigned to join the ranks of the Confederacy.

That said, many of the actual facts of the case seem to have been "stretched."

First, and not subject to debate, was Robert E. Lee's West Point record.

He was an exceptional cadet and graduated at the relatively young age of twenty-two without ever having received a single demerit . . . but he was not first in his class. He was second in a class of forty-six.

Grant also attended West Point (though admittedly fourteen years later) and excelled in math and horsemanship, by no means a shabby accomplishment. His place at twenty-first of thirty-nine is far from being at the bottom of the class (a distinction that was attained by George Armstrong Custer, who graduated thirty-fourth out of a class of thirty-four).

So Grant was actually in the middle of his class . . . and the awful truth of the matter is that from an academic and societal level, there really wasn't that wide a gulf between the two men in terms of their academic standing. Both were West Pointers, the elite of the elite—end of discussion.

Another myth concerns the gentility of Lee as opposed to the rude and crude Grant. Who can forget that Lee showed up in his dress best for the surrender at Appomattox Courthouse, while Grant was still in battlefield dress, trail dust and all.

One should recall that Lee had to convey an air of dignity and decorum—his side lost, and he owed to his men to provide the best spin possible.

For Grant, it was just anything to get the bloody war over and done with. Relatively speaking, he was just following orders from Washington.

Yes, he had won the war . . . but that was beside the point.

There is also a tendency to oversentimentalize both men.

Grant was often seen as the bloody butcher with a tendency

to drink who won by breaking the rules. (This is untrue—Grant did drink and did suffer from night terrors . . . but his military tactics were pragmatic to the extreme, and occasionally that included accepting that there would be heavy casualties in order to secure victory.)

Lee was viewed as a gentleman who played by the rules and only wound up on the Confederate side out of respect for his Virginia heritage. (This notion is also not quite true.)

Lee was a gentleman—a Southern gentlemen—and he didn't side with the South because of family pressures. He was a Southerner and not a reluctant Southerner at that.

He owned and trafficked in slaves and pursued all legal remedies at his disposal (including hiring slave catchers and ordering punishment for apprehended runaways) to secure his investment in this peculiar institution that was one of the backbones of the Southern economy. When he inherited additional slaves upon the death of his father-in-law, he put them to work despite a provision in the will that called for their emancipation. They were eventually freed, but only after they had contributed to the Lee family coffers.

He may have perceived himself as a gentleman farmer . . . but he was definitely a Southern gentleman farmer.

In reality, the two men were very similar. Both had their failings, but both were also of the crème de la crème.

Also both men reached the height of their careers at relatively the same stage of their lives—Lee as general in chief of the Confederate Army, and Grant as the commander in chief, the president of the United States.

The Emancipation Proclamation didn't free all the slaves

"If I could save the Union without freeing any slave, I would do it."

—Abraham Lincoln, August 22, 1862

O ur liberated and evolved educational system has finally instilled in the masses that the key issue of the Civil War was not really slavery, but the more subjective matter of states' rights. Moreover, the Union didn't rush in to start a war over the slavery issue or even over the states' rights issue, but entered in a response to the firing on Fort Sumter, an act akin to the attack on Pearl Harbor or the blowing up of the *U.S.S. Maine*.

"They started it—we'll settle it!"

Thus spake the North.

As commander in chief, President Lincoln had one goal to accomplish, and that was to reunite his nation at any cost.

The issue of slavery was beside the point.

Thus, when some of his generals—such as John C. Fremont and David Hunter—approached him to authorize their efforts to free all slaves in sectors under their command during the first year of the war, Lincoln refused.

Even when Lincoln took what could be considered positive action on the slavery issue, his dictum was couched in the same sort of legalese that permeated the Dred Scott decision, namely in the First Confiscation Act signed on August 6, 1861, which directed that the Union forces were enabled to seize private property used in the furthering of the rebellion.

The category "private property" included such things as ammunition, guns, horses, and, of course, slaves.

The direct result of this was that slaves who managed to make it to Union lines no longer had to be returned to their owners in compliance with various laws that were still believed to be in force (such as the Fugitive Slave Law).

The subjective result: slaves could still be viewed as property.

This is not to say that Lincoln favored the continuation of slavery. Quite the opposite. He and his Republican backers largely supported the abolitionist movement, but they also knew that it might cost them popular support and diminish their political power. Thus, the plan was to engineer a more gradual solution to the slavery problem through state-by-state reforms, with the further possibility of a federal buyout providing compensation to the slave owners in return for the emancipation of their private property.

However, as the war dragged on an opportunity presented itself.

Why not use the freeing of the slaves as an economic weapon against their rebellious foe? In addition to depleting their workforce on a practical level, it would also provide a wedge between the Confederacy and such foreign powers as Britain and France, from whom the rebels were seeking independent recognition as a sovereign state.

Lincoln drafted the proclamation carefully so as not to provoke anxiety in his Northern base of support (workers who feared that freed slaves would quickly replace them in the workforce and drive wages down) by exempting the border states. This move angered the abolitionists, who nonetheless continued to support his administration.

Lincoln finished his draft early in July 1862 and ran it by his most trusted cabinet members. William Seward, the secretary of state, advised that it should not be issued in a vacuum, and recommended that it not be announced until after a substantial Union victory.

The Battle of Antietam provided such a victory (despite the ineptitude of the Union commander on the scene, who managed to turn a slam dunk into a squeaker) and, thus, on September 22, 1862, he issued the preliminary proclamation freeing the slaves of the rebellious states, effective January 1, 1863.

Though this simple proclamation had little to no immediate practical effect on slaves, it did alter the perception of the goal of the Union forces in executing the war, as with every new victory they spread "freedom" farther and farther into the Confederacy (sort of like changing a rationale of prevention of the spread of weapons of mass destruction to one of spreading democracy in the Middle East).

The Union had latched onto a moral justification for war rather than a political justification, and along the way the slaves just happened to get freed.

Abner Doubleday was probably not the Father of Baseball

In the lovely town of Cooperstown there is a singular baseball museum featuring numerous tableaux of baseball greats, including Joe DiMaggio, Lou Gehrig, and Babe Ruth, as well as associated baseball personalities like Bud Abbott, Lou Costello, and George W. Bush.

Among the thirty-some exhibits is one of a Union Army Civil War officer studying some plans.

The museum is not the world-famous Baseball Hall of Fame (which lies farther down the same block) but rather the Heroes of Baseball Wax Museum, and the Union officer is none other than Abner Doubleday. While many consider Doubleday to have been baseball's founder, the tableau placard next to him clearly states that there is no evidence that he had anything to do with events that have led to his being designated the Father (or Inventor) of Baseball as we know it.

Now, being fair, a few points do need to be taken into account.

First, Doubleday did come from the general area of Cooperstown, New York. He was born in Ballston Spa, New York, in 1819, and he attended school in Auburn and Cooperstown before entering West Point, where he graduated with his commission in 1842.

Doubleday soon acquired a reputation as a truly upstanding military officer who forswore drinking, cursing, and tobacco, and served with distinction in both the Mexican War and the campaign against the Seminole Indians.

He was there when the first shots were fired at the opening of the Civil War at Fort Sumter and saw action in the Shenandoah Valley, and at Bull Run, Antietam, Fredericksburg, and Gettysburg.

He retired from the military in 1873 and settled in New Jersey.

Doubleday went on to publish two major works on the Civil War: *Reminiscences of Forts Sumter and Moultrie in 1860–'61* (1876), and *Chancellorsville and Gettysburg* (1882), the latter being a volume of the series *Campaigns of the Civil War.* (Originally published between 1881 and 1883, only twenty years after the beginning of the war; this series presented a concise and vivid account of the battles that composed the American Civil War by participants and contemporary witnesses to the conflict.) He also wrote numerous letters and was indeed considered to be quite literate and conversant on the various incidences of his life.

There is no record that the subject of baseball ever came up.

So how did he ever get the moniker the Father of Baseball?

As with many mistakes, the blame falls to a committee—in this case a special baseball commission, the Spalding Commission, who accepted as fact the testimony of a boyhood friend of Doubleday's by the name of Albert Graves. Graves claimed that Abner had set up the rules of the game in Cooperstown in 1839, which was "verified" by the discovery of the so-called "Doubleday baseball."

The salient and definitive points of the not-Doubleday argument are:

- He was not at Cooperstown in 1839.

- He never referred to the game in his writings.

- He never claimed that he invented it.

- His "famous person" extended obituary in the *New York Times* never mentioned baseball.

In Shakespeare's words, "Some have greatness thrust upon them."

There is little doubt that Doubleday was indeed a great man, but the Father of Baseball? Exceptionally doubtful.

It was an honor he never sought and indeed never deserved.

So then who *does* deserve this distinction?

A name that has recently received a great deal of support concerning this matter is Alexander Cartwright, Jr. In 1845 Cartwright supposedly devised the first set of rules and regulations for the game when he was a member of the New York Knickerbocker Base Ball Club. Under scrutiny, however, this claim to fame is probably as specious as the one attributed to Doubleday.

Nonetheless, based on his war record alone, Doubleday deserves a place among the pantheon of great American heroes.

The fact that he is primarily remembered for something he didn't and never took credit for is probably irrelevant.

Founder of Baseball

While we are all proud of our founder, baseball has to consider the long-term brand strategy. Now Marketing is hot on this Civil War hero guy Doubleday. Hell, even his name sounds like a promotional event…

Baseball's birthplace was probably not Cooperstown, New York

Fly Creek is a small village roughly three miles from Cooperstown, New York.

In a dusty old attic in an age-worn trunk, an antique homemade baseball was discovered that would eventually acquire the historic moniker the "Doubleday baseball," named after Abner Doubleday.

This ball was eventually acquired by a Cooperstown philanthropist who decided to have a museum established in town to showcase it and other baseball artifacts. His efforts coincided with a more established campaign to inaugurate a Baseball Hall of Fame in Cooperstown, New York, to commemorate the alleged hundredth anniversary of the game. On June 12, 1939, National League president Ford Frick, baseball commissioner Kenesaw Mountain Landis, and William Harridge cut the ribbon to open what is now Cooperstown's greatest claim to fame.

Why Cooperstown?

The evidence of the Doubleday baseball, the findings of the Mill Commission (which had been set up to look into the matter back in 1905), and the more than slight influence of that Cooperstown philanthropist who wanted to have the home of fame and glory in his own backyard.

Thus, Cooperstown became the birthplace of baseball, a more than slightly erroneous moniker at best.

Cooperstown could be the birthplace only if one were to believe the now discredited Abner Doubleday-as-inventor myth.

If that were truly the case, how does one account for records of a similar sort of game being played in Massachusetts in the late 1700s? Or what about the similarity of the game to the variation on the cricket, called rounders, that had an evolving set of rules that may or may not have reached their apex of evolution under Alexander Cartwright when he played a form of the game with the New York Knickerbockers?

One theory is that the advent of American nationalism and arrogance had something to do with it.

Baseball needed to be a truly American game with a great American as its originator, rather than just a slight deviation of a popular British game.

So just as George Washington was said to have chopped down the cherry tree, Doubleday was given credit for the game, and its birthplace was at least temporarily affixed at Cooperstown.

And even though the facts have largely discredited this entire case, for most Americans Cooperstown, the home of the National Baseball Museum and Hall of Fame, will always be the game's native ground.

The Awful Truth

is

That These Famous
Tough-Guy Actors

James Cagney,

Sean Connery,

&

Christopher Walken

All Started Out
as Chorus Boys

Edward Bulwer-Lytton of "It was a dark and stormy night" fame was the bestselling novelist of his time

Today he is remembered for the eponymous contest associated with the memorable opening line "It was a dark and stormy night."

Indeed, the aim of the annual Bulwer-Lytton Fiction Contest ("where www means wretched writers welcome"), sponsored by the English Department at San Jose State University, is to come up with the worst possible opening sentence for a novel.

The full quotation by Bulwer-Lytton (from the novel *Paul Clifford*, published in 1830) reads: "It was a dark and stormy night; the rain fell in torrents—except at occasional intervals, when it was checked by a violent gust of wind which swept up the streets (for it is in London that our scene lies), rattling along the housetops, and fiercely agitating the scanty flame of the lamps that struggled against the darkness."

And ever since those first seven words were procured by a certain literary beagle (created by Charles Schulz) as the opener for his novel de jour, Bulwer-Lytton has become the icon for overly written, overly melodramatic prose, and talentless neophyte novelists.

But the awful truth is that Bulwer-Lytton doesn't even come close to deserving such infamy, and was indeed considered to be a major talent in his day, earning both a certain measure of literary success among his peers as well as commercial success among the reading public. His versatility allowed his works to span many genres (including science fiction, heroic fantasy, and detective novel—all of which were just barely coming onto the scene) and perhaps even founded the so-called "school of crime fiction," dealing with the outsiders and exiles of London's criminal underworld.

Edward George Bulwer-Lytton, 1st Baron Lytton, was the youngest son of General William Earle Bulwer of Heydon Hall and Wood Dalling, and of Elizabeth Barbara Lytton, daughter of Richard Warburton Lytton of Knebworth, Hertfordshire. His first publication, a book of poems, came out in 1820 when he was not yet seventeen. He later branched out to the dramatic form, essays, short stories, and finally the novel.

According to John Juliet of the University of Salford:

> Bulwer wrote novels in many different styles: the "silver fork" novel *Pelham* (1828) was, according to John Sutherland, "the most popular and most often reprinted fashionable novel of the century" (*Times Literary Supplement*, July 28, 2000); his Newgate novel *Paul Clifford* (1830) is often seen as the first in this school of crime fiction; he consistently wrote historical novels (e.g., *Rienzi* [1835]), and claims have been made for him as the father of the English detective novel (e.g., *Night and Morning* [1841]), science fiction (e.g., *The Coming Race* [1871]), the fantasy novel (e.g., *A Strange Story* [1862]), the thriller, the domestic realistic novel (e.g., *The Caxtons* [1849]), the metaphysical novel, and the *bildungsroman*. He also wrote highly successful plays such as *Richelieu* (1839) and *Money* (1840).

Particularly popular were his well-researched historical novels such as *The Last Days of Pompeii* and *Harold: Last of the Saxon Kings*. He was even widely considered to be the heir of the mantle of Sir Walter Scott, and in 1853 he received the largest sum ever paid to a novelist at the time by his publisher George Routledge.

Beyond his commercial success he is also considered to have been a major influence on Edgar Allan Poe, and a personal influence and perhaps critical mentor to his contemporaries such as William Thackeray and Charles Dickens. He is credited with coining such memorable phrases as:

- "the pursuit of the almighty dollar"
- "the great unwashed"
- "the pen is mightier than the sword"

Bulwer-Lytton also pursued a career in politics and served in Parliament for nine years, and then later for fourteen years (having taken a break to focus more time on his literary career), resulting in his eventually being awarded a peerage as Baron Lytton of Knebworth.

Accepting the fact that his prose is definitely old-fashioned by today's standards (though the same can be said about his contemporaries Dickens and Anthony Trollope), and that his sheer productivity might call into question his quality (Does anyone wonder what the critical reception of the complete works of Danielle Steel or James Patterson will be one hundred years hence?), the infamy and ridicule heaped upon the name of this highly successful writer of the nineteenth century seems to be ill deserved indeed.

Unfortunately, the awful truth is that if not for the existence of the contest, it is entirely possible that the name Bulwer-Lytton might be all but forgotten, despite its earned stature among the classic writers of his time.

The Democratic Party was *the* party of segregation

he Democratic Party had its origins in the 1790s under the monikers "Democratic Republicans" or "Jeffersonian Republicans." The name was soon shortened to "Democrats" during the presidency of man of the people (provided you were white and male), Andrew Jackson.

The Republican Party emerged in the 1850s, composed largely of dissident groups concerned over the issues that would eventually lead to the coming of the Civil War. This party evolved into the antislavery-oriented party that backed Abraham Lincoln, making him the first modern Republican president of the United States. He was mythologized as the great freer of slaves, and led national Republican victories that enabled the groundwork for the Reconstruction era.

It was roughly at this juncture that it became simplistically obvious that the Democratic Party was seen as pro-South/states' rights/segregation, while the Republican Party (also called the Grand Old Party or simply the GOP) was viewed as the party of Lincoln and therefore the progenitor of the war that had been waged against the South, states' rights, and slavery.

With the exception of the presidency of Grover Cleveland, the Republicans had secured the executive branch under their control up until the World War I era. The Democratic Party maintained and grew its power base in Congress mainly by locking up large voting blocks in the South that were still bitter about the war, and even more bitter about Reconstruction.

However, by 1877 the Democratic Party had regained control of the Southern states, in effect ending any progress on Reconstruction. Moreover, the strides forward that blacks had made, such as holding political offices, voting, and moving toward participating as equal members of society were quickly reversed on the local level, defying legislation that had been set in motion on the federal level. With the Democrats in power, the South gradually reimposed racially discriminatory laws securing two main objectives—the disenfranchisement of the blacks and their segregation from white society. These Jim Crow laws utilized a variety of methods to stop blacks from voting, including poll taxes (fees charged at the voting booth that were too expensive for most blacks) and literacy tests, which required that voters be able to read to vote (since it had been illegal to teach a slave how to read, most adult former slaves were still illiterate).

The Democrats on the state level, and with the blessing of their congressmen in Washington, effectively began to create a segregated society that separated blacks and whites in almost every sphere of life. They passed laws that created separate schools and separate public facilities that allowed for an explicit discrimination on the basis of race, thus disadvantaging the non-whites and preventing them from moving up in society through substantial self-improvement.

This approach was further sanctioned by the Supreme Court in its decision *Plessy vs. Ferguson* (1896).

And all along, these programs and laws were fostered by Democratic political machines in the South, which were further protected by other party machines in the North that might disagree fundamentally on the moral issues involved yet offered their own benign blessing in the name of states' rights.

In all fairness it should be noted that there were many Republican supporters of these segregation programs . . . but given the Republicans' relative lack of power in the pertinent areas of the country, the "blame" must pragmatically be left squarely at the feet of the Democrats, the erstwhile party of segregation.

After World War II and the allegedly enlightened reign of Franklin Delano Roosevelt, certain progressive Democrats, however, such as then president Harry S Truman, began to further an agenda against segregation with such early initiatives as the desegregation of the military.

This led to a major split in the party that indeed jeopardized Truman's chances for reelection.

The States' Rights Democratic Party (also known as the Dixiecrats) was a short-lived splinter group that broke from the Democratic Party in 1948 in opposition to racial integration and in favor of the Jim Crow laws and racial segregation. The party slogan was "Segregation Forever!" On Election Day 1948, the Strom Thurmond–led Dixiecrat ticket carried the previously solid Democratic states of Louisiana, Mississippi, Alabama, and South Carolina, receiving 1,169,021 popular votes and 39 electoral votes. Everyone thought the split in the Democratic Party in the 1948 election would guarantee a victory for the Republican nominee, Thomas E. Dewey of New York, but it actually resulted in Truman's reelection in an upset (and the famous DEWEY DEFEATS TRUMAN headline). After the election, the defecting Democrats were reintegrated into the party without any repercussions for their actions.

Thurmond was eventually elected to the Senate as a Democrat and continued his support of racial segregation with the longest filibuster ever on the Senate floor, speaking for twenty-four hours and eighteen minutes in an unsuccessful attempt to derail the Civil Rights Act of 1957, before changing parties in 1964.

The Civil Rights Act of 1964 finally was passed during the Lyndon Johnson administration. The House of Representatives held more than seventy days of public hearings, during which some 275 witnesses offered nearly six thousand pages of testimony. At the end of this process, the House passed the bill by a 290 to 130 vote. A solid majority of senators also favored passage, but a two-thirds majority was needed to halt the inevitable filibuster (the consistent bane of civil rights legislation), which did not occur until June 10, 1964. That filibuster lasted for fifty-seven days, during which time the Senate could conduct virtually no other business. The act eventually passed, however, ushering in a new era of proposed equality and a sense of dividedness in the Democratic Party.

Several of the prominent Democrats who supported segregation eventually left the party to assume Republican affiliations in Congress. But one prominent politician who remained in the party (despite presidential runs as an Independent) was George Wallace, governor of Alabama. Wallace famously proclaimed, "Segregation now, segregation tomorrow, segregation forever!" as he stood at the schoolhouse door in 1963 at the University of Alabama and confronted federal authorities when they attempted to enroll black students. (Note: Wallace's support was not limited to the South, as evidenced by his Michigan primary victory in 1972.)

Another noted Democrat/Dixiecrat who remained within the party was Senator Robert Byrd of West Virginia, who went on to serve as Senate Democratic leader from 1977 to 1989, despite the fact that he was a former member of the Ku Klux Klan, and had filibustered against the Civil Rights Act in 1964. Byrd has since apologized for what many construe to be his sins of the past, and he is still serving in the Senate as of the writing of this book.

Lyndon Johnson is said to have predicted, as he signed the 1964 Civil Rights Act into law, that the Democratic Party would be demographically weakened by his support of the legislation, saying, "There goes the South for a generation."

Given the past few elections, it would appear that he grossly underestimated Southern memories, and the segregation legacy that had been democratically fostered in the South for so many years.

Now I'm sure if Miss Borden says that it was a misunderstanding,
then I'm sure it was a simple misunderstanding…

Lizzie Borden was found innocent

Lizzie Borden took an axe
And gave her mother forty whacks.
And when she saw what she had done
She gave her father forty-one.

For most of the twentieth century, after schoolchildren had outgrown Mother Goose, and before they moved on to the racy variations on the classic limerick that begins "There once was a man from Nantucket," this four-line lyrical evocation of the most brutal murder in the history of Fall River, Massachusetts, was one of the most popularly memorized bits of poetry.

But there's a problem.

It's erroneous.

Mrs. Abby Durfee Grey Borden received only nineteen blows from the axe, and she was Lizzie's stepmother. The first Mrs. Borden, Lizzie's mother, Sarah Morse Borden, died when Lizzie was only two.

And Mr. Andrew Jackson Borden had been the recipient of only ten blows.

That makes three major factual errors in four lines of poetry.

A fourth discrepancy in this poetic account is of a less nit-picking variety.

According to the American judicial system that tried Lizzie

for this most heinous of crimes, Lizzie never took up the axe against her parents.

Lizzie Borden was found innocent and acquitted of the crime in 1893, after the criminal judicial proceedings that were undoubtedly billed as "the trial of the century."

Lizzie and her older sister, Emma, resided with their father and his second wife (along with a housekeeper named Bridget Sullivan) at 92 Second Street in Fall River, Massachusetts, in a house befitting the well-to-do banker and his family. Both girls were considered unmarriageable spinsters past their prime, and rumors pervaded the town that there was a significant amount of friction between the girls and their father's second wife.

On August 4, 1892, while Emma was out of town, Mr. and Mrs. Borden were found slain by Lizzie and the maid.

Lizzie quickly notified the authorities and sought help from the neighbors before approaching the bodies. (It should be noted that none of the witnesses at the time ever noticed or recalled any bloody traces on Lizzie's hands or dress as might befit someone who had just engaged in a homocidal fury resembling the one that had been brought to bear on the victims.)

A coroner's inquest revealed that the two victims had been cranially cleaved and bludgeoned by an axelike weapon, and that there was apparently a gap of close to two hours between the murders, suggesting that the assailant was not pressed for time nor worried about being interrupted or discovered by some other member of the household.

Suspicion immediately fell on the "odd woman spinster" Lizzie, and a case was mounted against her, largely on the basis of circumstantial evidence and prejudice.

The trial was convened on June 5, 1893, and lasted two weeks, filled with gory demonstrations, exhibitions, and innuendos.

The jury deliberated for a little over an hour and came back with a verdict of not guilty, at which point Lizzie returned home with her sister, sold the family house, and moved into another of the town's mansions, where she spent the rest of her days.

Despite her being cleared in the court of law, there seems always to have been a presumption of guilt surrounding Lizzie, and a cloud of suspicion followed her for the rest of her days.

The four-line ditty (above) was only one of the many that newspapers ran.

The following poem by A. L. Bixby was available in newspapers even as the jury was evaluating evidence and testimony:

> *There's no evidence of guilt,*
> *Lizzie Borden,*
> *That should make your spirit wilt,*
> *Lizzie Borden;*
> *Many do not think that you*
> *Chopped your father's head in two,*
> *It's so hard a thing to do,*
> *Lizzie Borden.*
> *You have borne up under all,*
> *Lizzie Borden.*
> *With a mighty show of gall,*
> *Lizzie Borden;*
> *But because your nerve is stout*
> *Does not prove beyond a doubt*
> *That you knocked the old folks out,*
> *Lizzie Borden.*

Indeed, many of her accusers and detractors continued to doubt her innocence. Because the case was never solved and because she was the sole person ever to be charged with the crime, these facts have taken precedence in the public mind in a way that her acquittal never did . . . and each anniversary a summation in the local papers of that most heinous slaying in Fall River history only succeeded in further promulgating the misconception of her culpability.

Lizzie Borden died of complications from gallbladder surgery in 1927 at the age of sixty-six, thirty-four years after her acquittal. Her estate was divided among those friends and servants who stayed loyal to her over the years, along with a considerable donation to the Animal Rescue League of Fall River, per her last will and testament.

The myth of her guilt, and its four lines of poetic misrepresentation continue to live on. Indeed, even the Fall River tourist bureau seems to have encouraged this myth of guilt, with municipal signs for Fall River bearing the silhouette of a spinster bearing an axe.

"Under God" has not always been in the Pledge of Allegiance

"**I** pledge allegiance to the flag of the United States of America and to the Republic for which it stands, one nation under God, indivisible, with liberty and justice for all."

In recent years there has been a great deal of tongue wagging in Congress and the courts over the argument of whether or not the words "under God" belong in the Pledge of Allegiance.

There is, of course, one faction that would like to see all references to God removed from all official government and national matters, citing the constitutional directive of a clear separation of church and state. The clause reads:

"Congress shall make no law respecting an establishment of religion, or prohibiting the free exercise thereof; or abridging the freedom of speech, or of the press; or the right of the people peaceably to assemble, and to petition the Government for a redress of grievances."

And since it was Congress that officially added "under God" to the Pledge, the argument is that it should be removed on the basis of constitutional grounds.

Such a case (where a father sued on behalf of his daughter concerning the recitation of the Pledge in her school) was indeed dismissed by the Supreme Court in 2004, sidestepping many of the related issues of the case on the basis of available legal technicalities.

On the other side, there is a faction that maintains that the so-called founding fathers were deeply Christian men who fully intended that God have a role in all matters governmental or otherwise, and that the Pledge should not be tampered with, lest these founders' original intent be dishonored.

The major problem with this argument is that the founders did not conceive of the Pledge itself, nor has the Pledge itself been free of evolution in its lifetime.

Indeed, as originally drawn up, the so-called Pledge of Allegiance did not include the words "under God."

The Pledge was conceived and written as part of a national schools program by Francis Bellamy, the cousin of visionary Utopian philosopher and novelist Edward Bellamy, author of *Looking Backward*.

It read: "I pledge allegiance to my Flag and the Republic for which it stands; one nation indivisible, with liberty and Justice for all," and it appeared in print for the first time on September 8, 1892, in a periodical titled *The Youth's Companion*.

The profoundly Socialist leanings of its author were conveniently ignored, and the Pledge was soon embraced by all major factions of American society.

We now jump ahead to 1953, the beginnings of the cold war, the era of the Red Scare, and the first Republican presidential administration since the era of Democratic dominance that was ushered in by Franklin Delano Roosevelt. Congress was being lobbied hard by Catholic organizations, such as the Knights of Columbus, veterans' groups like the American Legion, and Red-baiting media monopolies like that of Hearst, that an affirmation of faith was a necessary part of our war against "godless communism." It was pointed out that various "red" and "pinko" (Communist and Socialist) groups had adopted similar oaths and orations that sounded an awful lot like the Pledge (not surprising, given the Socialist parentage of its author).

As a result, a bill was introduced to add the words "under God" to the Pledge, which would now be codified as the following:

"I pledge allegiance to the flag of the United States of America and to the Republic for which it stands, one nation under God, indivisible, with liberty and justice for all."

President Dwight D. Eisenhower signed the bill into law on June 14, 1954, with the clear intention of distancing the United States principles from those of the godless Communists who might at any moment threaten us with extinction through the use of their atomic weapons.

Thus, not only did the founding fathers have nothing to do with the Pledge, its original author was the exact sort of individual for whom the 1954 alteration and legislation was intended to distance it from, under God/god and/or whoever.

The Awful Truth

is
That the First
Major Motion Pictures
Solely Helmed by
Acclaimed Filmmakers

Francis Ford Coppola,
Martin Scorsese,

&

Robert Altman

Were

Dementia 13 *(a slasher film)*

Who's That Knocking at My Door?

(a coming-of-age film whose mantra is "Good girls don't")

&

Countdown *(a science fiction film)*

Harry Frazee actually came out ahead on the Babe Ruth deal

I t was said to have been the instigation of the Red Sox curse, the curse of the Bambino, and the irrational explanation of why, for most of the twentieth century, the Boston Red Sox failed to win the World Series.

On a cold January 5, 1920, Babe Ruth was sold by Red Sox owner Harry Frazee to the New York Yankees for $125,000 and a $350,000 mortgage on Fenway Park by Yankee owner Jacob Ruppert.

Ruth's record with the Red Sox was indeed impressive.

In four years as a pitcher, Ruth was 78 and 40. In 1919, he batted .322 with twenty-nine home runs, playing left field for the Red Sox.

But unfortunately, all was not paradise at Fenway.

Frazee was financially overextended and had problems with debts and his partners. His team was becoming less competitive (with the exception of Ruth), and he had other interests, ventures, and obligations as well—some of which had the potential to yield him far greater rewards.

And his star player George Herman "Babe" Ruth was also a problem.

First off, he was a pitcher, and a damn good one at that, but pitchers can't play every day, and as has been seen on numerous contemporary occasions (e.g., superstar Kevin Brown's recent lackluster tenure at the Yankees and various stars of yesteryear who continue to play rather than accepting their rightful place at the MLB glue factory), pitchers have a tendency to become "over the hill" with very little notice.

It was more advantageous for Frazee to get rid of the Babe while he could still get a good price for him as a pitcher.

Ruth was also less than pleased with his situation at the Sox, and he felt he was being drastically underpaid.

Why have a dissatisfied player poisoning the public and further devaluing the franchise?

From a purely business standpoint, Frazee made the right decision, no matter what the majority of twentieth-century Red Sox fans might think.

Besides that, Frazee's real passion was the theater.

Born in Peoria, Illinois, an usher, box-office man, and theatrical agent by age sixteen, Frazee came to New York in 1909 and quickly left his heart firmly ensconced in the theater district. He backed a few shows and with the profits built the Longacre Theater in 1913. He also eventually bought the Harris Theater and promptly renamed it after himself.

Though not every show he backed succeeded, he did indeed make more money in show business than he would ever realize in the business of baseball.

American pop culture has held that Frazee used the money from the Ruth sale to back the highly successful musical *No, No, Nanette* . . . but recently belligerent Boston fans have been all too eager to debase Frazee's reputation for bringing on the curse, pointing out that the musical in question didn't open on Broadway until five years after the blackest of all baseball transactions, thus implying that Frazee's judgment did not even pay off as a smart business move (even if one were to divorce one's loyalty from the great American pastime).

In this case the facts are right, but the conclusion is wrong.

No, No, Nanette did not debut on Broadway until 1925. However, at around the same time that Frazee was dealing away Ruth, he was also producing a new play on Broadway. It was *My Lady Friends* by Frank Mandel, and it had a minorly successful run until the death of one of its stars led to its early closing.

Still, the show earned some marginal profits on the road and with the advent of a London production.

Frazee was still not satisfied with its level of success, and he continued to pour the profits back into the show, eventually commissioning songs to turn it into a musical. Two of these songs would become hit standards of Broadway music: "I Want to Be Happy" and "Tea for Two."

When the musical version eventually made its way to Broadway in 1925, after a successful out-of-town tour, it had a new title—*No, No, Nanette* (based on the play *His Lady Friends*, the title to which *My Lady Friends* was changed when it opened in London).

The musical netted more than $20,000 a week for quite a while, and it has gone on to become one of the classics of the American musical theater, as well as a landmark of Broadway success stories.

Frazee's investment, or, rather, his redirection of funds, paid off.

In baseball terms, he definitely hit a home run, no matter what irate Boston fans might think.

Al Capone was a convicted felon prior to his arrest for income tax evasion

> "He remained immune from prosecution for his multitudinous murders (including the St. Valentine Day Massacre in 1929 when his gunners, dressed as policemen, trapped and killed eight of the Bugs Moran bootleg outfit in a Chicago garage), but was brought to book, finally, on the comparatively sissy charge of evasion of income taxes amounting to around $215,000."
>
> —from the New York Times *obituary of Al Capone*

Everybody knows that "Scarface Al" Capone was sent away for tax evasion, and it has been in the public mind since then that this was the only crime for which he was ever convicted.

Yet he was still considered Public Enemy #1 in Chicago, despite the fact that everyone knew where to find him.

He wasn't wanted for a crime—that would have taken an indictment, and evidence, and a compelling case that didn't exist or wasn't available to the authorities at the time.

Al Capone wasn't wanted for a crime—the authorities just *wanted* him to go away, and tax evasion provided that opportunity.

Capone is alleged to have said, "The income tax law is a lot of bunk. The government can't collect legal taxes from illegal money."

The Supreme Court disagreed, and in 1927 in *United States*

vs. Sullivan a unanimous Court held that the Fifth Amendment did not protect a bootlegger in not filing an income tax return because the filing would have disclosed the illegality in which he was engaged. "It would be an extreme if not an extravagant application of the Fifth Amendment to say that it authorized a man to refuse to state the amount of his income because it had been made in crime" (stated Justice Oliver Wendell Holmes, Jr. in the lead opinion).

Two years later in a federal court in Chicago, after nearly nine hours of deliberation, the jurors found Capone guilty of three felonies and two misdemeanors, relating to his failure to pay and/or file his income taxes between 1925 and 1929. Judge James H. Wilkerson sentenced Al Capone to serve eleven years in prison and to pay $80,000 in fines and court costs.

The Feds had finally gotten their man and placed Capone behind bars.

But the awful truth is that this was neither Capone's first arrest nor even his first conviction. Scarface Al had even served time before this and not just an overnight in a jail cell while he waited for his mouthpiece to spring him.

He was already a convicted felon.

The justice system had already had a clear shot at him.

Nonetheless, prior to his altercation with the IRS he was free as a bird.

Capone's first arrest was in 1916, a disorderly conduct charge early in his career while he was still in his teens and working for Frankie Yale of the Five Points Gang in New York. True, it was small stuff, but it counted nonetheless.

His real career didn't get off the ground until he got to Chicago, where he quickly rose through the ranks, establishing himself as their kingpin of crime, making prosecutions difficult due to his active campaign of intimidation and bribery that some say reached as high as Mayor William Hale Thompson's office . . . but that wasn't what got in the way of his being arrested and convicted of federal crimes.

It was the Feds' own guidelines that caused the problem.

The investigative jurisdiction of the Federal Bureau of Investigation during the 1920s and early 1930s was more limited than it is now, and the gang warfare and depredations of the period were not within the Bureau's investigative authority. Capone's crimes were considered the province of local jurisdiction.

That said, the Feds still managed to arrest and convict him of several charges prior to the IRS case.

On March 27, 1929, Capone was arrested by agents for contempt of court, an offense for which the penalty could be one year and a $1,000 fine. He posted $5,000 bond and was released, and on February 28, 1931, he was found guilty in federal court on the charge and sentenced to six months in Cook County Jail.

Between his charge for that and his conviction, he was arrested and convicted on another charge. On May 17, 1929, Al Capone and his bodyguard were arrested in Philadelphia for carrying concealed deadly weapons. Within sixteen hours they had been sentenced to terms of one year each. Capone served his time and was released in nine months for good behavior on March 17, 1930.

It, therefore, wasn't the fact that he was arrested and convicted that made the IRS case so sweet; it was the fact that it was sending him away for a long time—and was even making money on the deal. (The fact that Capone left jail a broken and sick man was just icing on the cake.)

The pursuit of justice is one thing.

The pursuit of back taxes is another, and for the Feds a criminal conviction for murder, robbery, et cetera, might not have been as advantageous for all those on the arresting end, which makes you wonder if this were the real reason they hadn't put him away before that point.

I understand they're work related, but
I still need a receipt for the tommy gun.

FDR committed numerous impeachable offenses

Franklin Delano Roosevelt is considered by many to be the greatest American president of the twentieth century, and he consistently ranks in the top five of all U.S. presidents in polls and surveys.

His four terms as chief executive changed the course of government as we know it, the U.S. economy, and the role of the United States in the world beyond our shores, ushering in an era when we would emerge as the first true world power.

In addition to his political accomplishments, he also had a rapport with the masses, well loved and respected for his own personal triumphs over adversity.

Yet it doesn't even take a close examination to determine that many of the actions he took as president could have resulted in his impeachment and dismissal from office.

First question: What exactly is meant by "impeachment?"

The U.S. Constitution states in article II, section 4: "The President, Vice President and all civil Officers of the United States, shall be removed from Office on Impeachment for, and Conviction of, Treason, Bribery, or other high Crimes and Misdemeanors."

An actual definition of what the founding fathers meant by "other high crimes and misdemeanors" is not clear.

The dictionary defines the word *impeachment* as follows: "To charge (a public official) with improper conduct in office before a proper tribunal."

However, when we get down to practical matters and specifics, an impeachable offense might be as simple as immoral turpitude or a gross violation of due process, but might not include an act that could be considered, under other circumstances, to be a felony.

A simple lie might be enough or it might not even be considered.

Of all forty-three presidents to date, three presidents have been confronted with impeachment proceedings, and none of them has been convicted and removed from office by the mandatory majority.

The first was brought against President Andrew Johnson in 1868 for his removal of Secretary of War Edwin Stanton in a direct violation of the Tenure of Office Act (the most specific case mounted to date). In the cases against Nixon and Clinton, on the other hand, though they involved very specific—one might even go so far as to say legalistic—matters, the charges themselves and the actual illegality of the matter were indeed much more general and/or amorphous (e.g., "abuse of power").

The fact that only three presidents have faced impeachment is more a matter of situational politics than actual actions and/or offenses (while having the opposition party in majority status in Congress is not an insignificant factor).

One might wish to make the argument that Franklin Delano Roosevelt, throughout his entire political career, purposely deprived the voting public of the facts concerning his health and physical condition, which indeed only worsened as his tenure in office progressed. That matter, however, is better reserved for TV's *The West Wing* rather than this discussion.

His health aside, the possibly impeachable offenses by FDR were far more significant than lying about sex or determining what the real meaning of the word *is* is.

Possibly the largest case for attempted "abuse of power" could made against FDR for his attempt to subvert the delicate balance of power that exists among our three branches of government. This plot involved an overt effort to stack the Supreme Court and undermine the conservative wing that seemed always to get in his way.

During 1937 the Court ruled that the National Recovery Act and some other pieces of New Deal legislation were unconstitutional. Roosevelt's response was to propose enlarging the Court so that he could appoint more sympathetic judges while encouraging some of the older, more conservative justices to retire. His proposal included the addition of several new judges (as many as six) to back up those over a certain age, thus pretty much guaranteeing the executive branch a controlling majority on every decision through their pet appointnments. Eventually Roosevelt was forced to abandon the plan, due to the hostile reaction from Congress, the press (the *Chicago Tribune* editorialized, "Shall the Supreme Court be turned into the personal organ of the President? . . . If Congress answers yes, the principle of an impartial and independent judiciary will be lost in this country"), and even those justices who might have been sympathetic to his legislative agenda.

Such clear overreaching and assumption of authority could indeed be considered as a possible "abuse of power."

His second, and more blatant, possible "abuse of power" involved his purposeful ignoring of the will of Congress in matters of foreign diplomacy.

In 1935, after Italy had invaded Abyssinia, Congress passed the Neutrality Act, applying a mandatory ban on the shipment of arms from the United States to any combatant nation. Roosevelt opposed the act on the grounds that it restricted his right as president to assist friendly countries, but he eventually signed it. In 1937 Congress passed an even more stringent act. When World War II came to Europe in 1939, FDR was eager to assist Britain and France, and he began a regular secret correspondence with Winston Churchill, in which the two freely discussed ways of circumventing the Neutrality Acts.

Many small-scale deals gave way to larger ones as the executive branch tried to assist the enemies of the Axis powers, right up to the 1941 Lend-Lease Agreement, which began to direct massive military and economic aid to Britain and then later to the Soviet Union.

In effect, despite the congressional Neutrality Acts, FDR had chosen a side in the war for America to support, and one might argue that in doing so he had usurped Congress's guaranteed power to declare war.

This infuriated various vocal members of such noninterventionist groups as America First.

Father Charles E. Coughlin, the noted radio priest and rabble-rouser, on September 9, 1940, even used the word *impeachment:*

> On previous occasions Congressmen have called for the impeachment of the President. On those occasions most citizens disagreed with the Congressmen.
>
> At length, however, an event has transpired which now marks Franklin D. Roosevelt as a dangerous citizen of the Republic—dangerous insofar as he has transcended the bounds of his Executive position.
>
> In plain language, without the knowledge or consent of Congress, he has denuded this country of thirty-six flying fortresses, either selling or giving them to Great Britain. By this action Franklin D. Roosevelt has torpedoed our national defense, loving Great Britain more than the United States. He has consorted with the enemies of civilization— through the continued recognition of Soviet Russia. He has deceived the citizens of the United States—telling the newspaper reporters, who are the people's eyes and ears at Washington, that he did not know the whereabouts of these flying fortresses. He has transcended the bounds of his Executive position—spurning the authority of Congress. He has invited the enmity of powerful foreign nations—on whose natural resources we depend for essential tin and rubber.
>
> Because he has encouraged the British government to reopen the Burma Road, and encouraged Britain to declare war on the German government, when Britain was unable to care for the English people—he stands revealed as the world's chief warmonger.

All these events, culminating with the transfer of these 36 flying fortresses without the consent of Congress, demand that he be impeached.

His concerns were further echoed by Senator Burton K. Wheeler of Montana on January 12, 1941, during debate in Congress:

The lend-lease-give program is the New Deal's triple-A foreign policy; it will plow under every fourth American boy. Never before have the American people been asked or compelled to give so bounteously and so completely of their tax dollars to any foreign nation. Never before has the Congress of the United States been asked by any President to violate international law. Never before has this nation resorted to duplicity in the conduct of its foreign affairs. Never before has the United States given to one man the power to strip this nation of its defenses. Never before has a Congress coldly and flatly been asked to abdicate.

If the American people want a dictatorship—if they want a totalitarian form of government and if they want war—this bill should be steam-rollered through Congress, as is the wont of President Roosevelt.

Approval of this legislation means war, open and complete warfare.

In the long run, that matter was finally taken out of FDR's hands by Japan's bombing of Pearl Harbor and Germany's declaration of war on the United States. In addition to being a retroactive justification for the steps that had been taken by the president, the official declaration and involvement in the war provided the necessary distraction that allowed FDR to remain free of impeachment worries, his legacy and prominence assured for years to come, provided we won World War II.

Which, under his leadership, we did, even if he himself did not survive to see it.

And, as a result, the four-term president who stretched the

lengths of executive power more than any of his predecessors set a model for established and entrenched (and, therefore, pragmaticly unassailable) authority that had to be immediately undercut by the Twenty-second Amendment in 1951:

> *No person shall be elected to the office of the President more than twice, and no person who has held the office of President, or acted as President, for more than two years of a term to which some other person was elected President shall be elected to the office of the President more than once.*

. . . thus assuring that a presidential reign as long as FDR's would never happen again.

There are more than a few detractors, usually on the far right of the Republican Party, who still argue that FDR should have been impeached, even if retroactively. The grounds range from the loony to the likely to the totally irresponsible, including such acts of "treason and high crimes as":

- provoking and facilitating an enemy attack on U.S. soil by purposely allowing the attack on Pearl Harbor in order to augment the official U.S. entry into the war

- allowing the United States to ally itself with an enemy power (the Soviet Union) and facilitate their development of nuclear weapons via the authorization of the transfer of supplies of uranium and soft water

- the selling out of American values at Yalta by allowing the Communists to take Eastern Europe

- the subsequent oppressing of said people behind the so-called Iron Curtain under Communist rule for the following four decades until they were liberated by the Republican savior Ronald Reagan

- numerous accounts of his engaging in alleged marital infidelities and fiscal favoritism, as well as other

entirely unsubstantiated rumors ranging from embezzlement to adultery and worse

But such claims are merely products of distorted partisan
posturing of President Roosevelt as part of the great Communist
conspiracy and an active pawn of the Red Menace. Besides which,
impeachment in his case would be totally unnecessary; it could
only result in his removal from office, an outcome already secured by his death in office.

The creation of Batman was not a solo project, no matter what the credit line says

I t's one of the most famous bylines in comic book history.

"Batman created by Bob Kane."

In an industry where collaboration was the general rule (artist with writer/scripter), Batman's creator credit always indicated a solo effort, unlike the Siegel and Shuster credit for Superman and the numerous Stan Lee and Jack Kirby credits for the marvelous heroes of the Marvel universe.

So why did Kane get sole credit on Batman?

Shrewd negotiating.

Given the "contractual" problems that had surfaced in their agreements with Jerry Siegel and Joe Shuster over Clark Kent's super alter ego, DC Comics was more than willing to legally and explicitly codify their relationship with Bob Kane concerning the Caped Crusader with an ongoing contractual relationship concerning future work and a guaranteed creator credit on all Batman material.

But the awful truth is that Batman was the product of several collaborations, both in genesis and ongoing execution.

The origin of "the origin of Batman," according to legendary comics' editor Julius Schwartz, is as follows:

I know that everyone has heard that Bob Kane (born Robert Kahn) is the creator of Batman from the character's debut in *Detective Comics* #27 in June of 1939. . . . The real story is that back in 1938, when *Superman* was a big hit, its editor—Vince Sullivan—wanted to try to duplicate its success with a similar sort of costumed hero. So Vince went to a young cartoonist named Bob Kane, and asked him to come up with a similar character. He even suggested that for inspiration he might look to a silent movie that featured a story about a bat. So off Bob went and came back with a rough sketch. Vince liked what he saw and told Bob to come back with the story.

Ergo, the original inspiration for Batman came from the editor of *Superman*—not Kane, giving the real stellar résumé of fatherhood to Vince Sullivan.

Now Bob Kane wasn't a storyteller. He was an illustrator, so he got his close friend Bill Finger—a rabid fan of the pulps, which featured numerous masked mystery heroes—to flesh out a storyline and background for *his* creation.

So the awful truth of the matter is Bob Kane may have drawn Batman, but it was Bill Finger who came up with the back story, the Wayne manor, Alfred the butler, and oh so many memorable villains.

So why didn't Bill Finger get a credit?

The comic company didn't have him under contract. It had the contract with Kane, and Kane subcontracted the writing to Finger without ever notifying the company.

Indeed, Bill Finger was only publicly outed as the real cocreator of the original character when Julie Schwartz took over the editorial reins of the series, describing its new incarnation this way: "Invigorated by a new look, Bob Kane has fashioned an extraordinary art job for 'Gotham Gang Line Up' inspired by the swell script of Bill Finger, who has written many of the classic Batman adventures of the past two decades."

That is believed to be the first actual Bill Finger credit on *Batman* in print; up to this point the general public saw only a credit for Bob Kane.

Nonetheless, Kane continued to receive solo credit even after he began to subcontract the art as well as the writing of the series.

Batman became his passive-participation bread and butter.

Kane went on to create a few other memorable characters for TV cartoon shows—including Courageous Cat, Minute Mouse, and Cool McCool—but none ever achieved the timeless heights of popularity of the Caped Crusader, whose parentage and ongoing evolution as an American pop-culture icon is actually the product of such other creative talents as Jerry Robinson, John Broome, Shelly Moldoff, Denny O'Neil, and countless other comic book luminaries.

Though it is now standard practice to credit the new artists and scripters on the comic, Kane still receives solo credit for the character's creation.

The Awful Truth

is
That These Famous
Cartoon Characters

The Announcer *on* Rocky &
Bullwinkle

The Announcer *on* Super Friends

&

Tigger & Dick Dastardly

Were Voiced by

William Conrad *(of* Cannon *and*
Jake and the Fatman)

Ted Knight *(of* The Mary Tyler
Moore Show *and* Too Close for
Comfort)

&

Paul Winchell *(inventor of the
artificial heart)*

The real reason he was known as the Birdman of Alcatraz.

The Birdman of Alcatraz never kept birds at Alcatraz

In 1955 a book titled *Birdman of Alcatraz* by Thomas E. Gaddis was published, documenting the curious case of Robert Stroud, an inmate at Alcatraz since December 1942, who, over the course of his close to a half century of incarceration in the American penal system, had become a self-taught ornithologist and a pioneer in the study and treatment of various bird diseases.

The book provided the basis for a 1962 film version of Stroud's story, with Burt Lancaster playing the sympathetic Birdman and garnering an Academy Award nomination for the role, and engendering an erstwhile petition drive to bring about the parole of Stroud. (Indeed, when a fellow inmate who knew Stroud heard about the drive from an outside visitor—the movie never having been shown at the prison—he was forced to conclude that if the majority of moviegoers actually met the man, they couldn't possibly want to pardon him because Stroud was nowhere near as attractive or as likable as the pearly-toothed Lancaster).

Lancaster didn't win the Oscar and Stroud didn't win parole, but the *Birdman of Alcatraz* became a permanent part of American pop culture.

The only problem, besides the fact that Stroud was no Burt Lancaster, was the misinformation of the title.

Stroud never kept birds at Alcatraz, and, for some reason, no one ever thought to change the title to the more accurate *Birdman of Leavenworth* (the penal institution that allowed him to pursue his winged interests during his stay).

Alcatraz was a maximum security installation whose penal population had included the likes of Al Capone and George "Machine Gun" Kelly. The day-in, day-out schedule was quite severe, and a rigid regimen of rules was duly enforced with extreme (some might say cruel) punishments as deterrents.

Alcatraz was not going to allow a "celebrity prisoner" any perks, so birds were definitely out of the question.

The only compromise was that Stroud was allowed to continue his research and writings via the prison library and to access journals and other birders of serious study via the mail (which was subject to the rigors of all inmate mail). This was, of course, contingent on Stroud behaving well, which was far from always the case, according to other inmates and guards who looked upon him as a disagreeable and degenerate inmate.

Indeed, if one excludes his obvious knack for ornithological study, there is not much positive that can be said about the Birdman.

Stroud was nineteen when he was convicted of killing an acquaintance named Charlie, whom he believed had beaten up his "girlfriend," a woman seventeen years his senior who was known to work as a dance hall girl and prostitute. (In the trial an implication was made that Stroud was her pimp, but no other charges were filed relating to this.) He was sentenced to twelve years at a local prison, where he soon proved himself to be a problem inmate. After an incident in which he stabbed a fellow prisoner, he was transferred to Leavenworth Federal Penitentiary in Kansas, where he confirmed his "problem status" by killing a guard in an altercation (the film version tries to cast this killing in a sympathetic light). This action resulted in his receiving a death sentence, which was then reduced to life imprisonment through political intercession at the highest level.

The life imprisonment sentence, however, was to be carried out as if he were still to be executed, which left him in segregation on death row for the duration of his sentence.

It was in segregation that he adopted his first bird and thus started his life of solitary study in the field of canaries and bird diseases with the indulgence of the Leavenworth warden and guards. The staff allowed him to keep birds in his cell and re-search avian pathology by means of correspondence with other experts, leading to his publication of two books—*Diseases of Canaries* and *Stroud's Digest on the Diseases of Birds*.

His ascent to a position as an authority in his field of study and a pioneer in a study that led to a cure for a strain of bird hem-orrhagic septicemia also led to a degree of unwanted attention to his exceptional status. He was, after all, a problem prisoner, with evident privileges far outreaching his station as an inmate in seg-regation. This attention eventually led to the removal of all of his birds and his subsequent transfer to Alcatraz.

On "the Rock," Stroud further alienated his warders by writ-ing a critical history of the American penal system, which he hoped to have published through the same venues he had used for his bird books.

The prison authorities succeeded in blocking the book by ban-ning such a publication by an inmate currently serving a sentence.

According to guards and inmates during Stroud's stay, the Birdman bristled at his lack of privileges, behaved in an antisocial manner, and often baited the warders with crude and irreverent behavior. Far from the soft-spoken intellectual portrayal by Burt Lancaster, the real Birdman was a hardened con with all of the usual maladjustments that made him unsuitable for the company of "civilized people." Whether his behavior had been reinforced by the cruelness of a life in segregation or was just the further blossoming of the soul of the man who had started his criminal inmate career with vice and homicide, it is impossible to tell.

Stroud served out his final days in a hospital wing in Missouri (from 1959 to 1963). All told, he had spent fifty-four of his seventy-three years in prison: twenty with birds in Leavenworth, none with birds in Alcatraz.

No one ever expected *Casablanca* to become a classic

*C*asablanca, the classic cinematic tale of love and patriotism, has earned itself a place on most people's top-ten lists of the greatest films ever made. Its fans claim Bogie and Bergman were never better and recite such lines as "I think this is the beginning of a beautiful friendship," "Here's looking at you, kid," and "We will always have Paris" as if they were texts on par with those by Shakespeare.

Some say it was destined to be a classic.

But the awful truth of the matter is that even those involved in the film were surprised by its success. To them, it was just another studio film done on a tight budget and rigorous schedule as performed by all of the usual suspects who just happened to be under contract at the time. In Roger Ebert's words "No one making *Casablanca* thought they were making a great movie. It was simply another Warner Bros. release. . . . Everyone involved in the film had been, and would be, in dozens of other films made under similar circumstances."

The basis for the film was a less-than-successful play titled *Everybody Comes to Rick's,* and the actual screenplay and ending of the film were not even written until well into the production, with many scenes not handed to the actors until hours before filming. Indeed, Ingrid Bergman had no idea who she was going to wind up with, Rick or Lazlo, until after that final scene was shot.

Many of the studio folk were concerned when they found out that the entire plot evolved around "letters of transit," which they

feared no one would have ever heard of. This was further complicated by the fact that letters of transit were never actually used in
the actual city of Casablanca at the time depicted . . . but, again,
since expectations were modest no one bothered to act on these
concerns. What the studio fold were concerned with was the
eventual international distribution of the film. They, therefore,
frequently requested changes to the script that might cast certain
European markets in a more flattering light . . . which of course
resulted in additional time-consuming rewrites.

George Raft was Jack Warner's choice for Rick, but a tiff with
producer Hal Wallis secured the part for Bogart, despite the fact
that he was not really seen as the romantic type. Hard-bitten, sure.
Menacing bad man, of course. Ladies man about town? Well, no,
not really . . . but since it was just another Warner film with modest expectations, the stakes weren't high, so why not gamble a little in the casting? It was only once shooting began that anyone
realized that Bogart was shorter than Bergman, thus resulting in
the need for clever camera work and staging to hide this fact.

The famous song "As Time Goes By" was supposed to be
changed to an original song composed for the picture, but time
and budget ran out.

And when filming was over, everybody moved on to their
next project. Ingrid Bergman cut her hair for *For Whom the Bell
Tolls*, thus rendering reshoots of key scenes impossible.

The film was good enough, and that was all that mattered.

As luck would have it, the Allies invaded Casablanca in real
life on November 8, 1942. Because the film was not due for release until spring, the studio considered changing the ending to
make it more up to date. Selznick requested a screening and informed Wallace:

Dear Hal:

Saw *Casablanca* last night. Think it is a swell movie and an all-
around job of picture making. Told Jack [Warner] as forcibly as I
could that I thought it would be a terrible mistake to change the
ending. . . . Knowing what they started with, I think the firm of

Epstein, Epstein and Koch did an expert piece of writing. Even though Rick's philosophy is in at least one instance word for word that of Rhett Butler.... I am most grateful to you and to Mike Curtiz for the superb handling of Ingrid. Thanks to you two, and of course to Ingrid, the part seems much better than it actually is....

> —*telegram from David O. Selznick to producer Hal Wallis, November 12, 1942*

Selznick recommended that it be released, unaltered, and as fast as possible. The studio agreed, and it premiered in New York shortly thereafter, on November 26. (It did not play in Los Angeles until its general release the following January, and hence competed against 1943 films for the Oscars, an eventuality that no one seemed concerned by as it was not considered *that* good a picture.)

The initial reviews reflected the studio's opinion with *Boxoffice* magazine assessing, "The story holds up well enough. . . . It is fair Bogart," pretty much what the studio heads were expecting—a nice, successful studio film that would show a profit.

What they got was much more than that.

Audiences latched onto it as *the* love story of World War II and flocked to the theater in droves. It was the perfect combination of the defeat of the Nazis and the dilemma that occurs when one is offered a second chance at love.

It was about the self-sacrifice that everybody endured during the war.

It struck a chord with America and, as a result, far surpassed the expectations of everybody connected with it.

If I had known it was going to be this big, I would have
held out for a piece of the merchandising rights.

It's a Wonderful Life was an initial disappointment

It has become a staple of the Christmas holiday season with multiple airings on all different networks, sometimes done in twenty-four-hour nonstop marathons.

It was the project that marked the return of Frank Capra and Jimmy Stewart to Hollywood after their World War II service, and included a glorious cast of Hollywood regulars: Donna Reed, Lionel Barrymore, Henry Travers, H. B. Warner, and Frank Faylen and Ward Bond (as two characters named Bert and Ernie).

Capra recalled in his memoirs: "A good man, ambitious. But so busy helping others, life seems to pass him by. Despondent. He wishes he had never been born. He gets his wish. Through the eyes of a guardian angel he sees the world as it would have been had he not been born. Wow! What an idea."

By now most people know the story of George Bailey, Bedford Falls, mean Mr. Potter, Clarence Odbody the Angel, and the new piece of Christmas mythology that "every time a bell rings an angel get his wings"; even if everyone hasn't actually sat through in a single sitting a viewing of the movie in its original, glorious black-and-white tones, they have no doubt seen one of the numerous takeoffs on its simple story, such as *Married with Children*'s *It's a Bundyfull Life*, Marlo Thomas's *It Happened One Christmas*, or MTV's animated version featuring Beavis and Butt-Head (there was even a foreign film starring Richard E. Grant titled *Franz Kafka's It's a Wonderful Life*).

Some might even be aware that Capra, Stewart, and the film itself were all nominated for Oscars.

But the awful truth of the matter is that regardless of its nominations it failed to draw enough box office even to cover its production costs. As a result, Capra's Liberty Films went under, and the rights to the film wound up reverting to Capra's distributor, RKO. Where *The Best Years of Our Lives,* the film that swept the Oscars that year, took in $11.3 million at the box office, *It's a Wonderful Life* garnered only $3.3 million (the film cost $3.78 million to make).

Though most reviews were kind, welcoming Stewart and Capra back after their service, they were barely laudatory (*The New Yorker* in particular vitiating its pixieish performance and dialogue, which bordered on "baby talk"), and audiences, having just survived a world war, were reluctant to embrace both the depressing world without George Bailey where everything was wrong, good people suffered, and only the rich got richer, or the saccharine sweet life where embezzlement (which in reality was theft) can easily be glossed over by the help of friends and a good old-fashioned potluck fund-raising drive.

Even more problematic, the red-hunting FBI took an interest in the film, citing its caricature of the Scrooge-like evil banker (Potter, as played by Barrymore) as anticapitalist and therefore pro-Communist, and its deification of the common man in the form of George Bailey, who must overcome adversity through an alliance with his fellow downtrodden citizens of Bedford Falls, as Marxist propaganda at its most insidious.

Though Stewart's career managed to get back on the "right" track, Capra's never did . . . at least not to the level it was before his wartime service.

And though *It's a Wonderful Life* ascended to the heights of popularity through repeated television showings, none of the initial folk who made it into such a classic ever received a cent from its earnings, due to the bankruptcy of Liberty Films.

Fidel Castro was never scouted by any major U.S. baseball team

In the TV series *Head of the Class,* the hip teacher played by Howard Hesseman asks his class of stuck-up braniacs about what role baseball played in the Cuban missile crisis, then proceeds to engage the class in a discussion about the unforeseen ramifications of a single act, a subject matter dear to the hearts of all geeky aficionados of alternate histories.

The connection he was referencing concerns the story that, at one point in the 1940s, during Fidel Castro's college days, he was scouted by a major U.S. baseball team (accounts conflict—some say the Yankees, other say the Senators) and given a tryout as a pitcher. Fidel went, gave a lackluster performance, and was basically told that though his stuff was fine for Cuba, he did not have what it takes to make it in the big-time baseball leagues of the United States of America.

As the legend goes, the discouraged Castro went home and became a revolutionary, forever holding a grudge against the U.S. purveyors of America's favorite pastime.

Thus, if Fidel had made the cut, the thinking goes, Cuba would never have gone Communist, ergo, no Cuban missile crisis, and, perhaps more important, no U.S. ban on Cuban cigars.

Definitely a neat little story.

It even makes Fidel Castro look a bit sympathetic. After all, he wouldn't have been the first young person to embrace the act of revolution, having had all of his dreams (e.g., playing in the big leagues) shattered in the blink of an eye.

A neat little story.

But, of course, the awful truth is that that is all it is, just a neat little story that never actually happened.

The relevant facts not in dispute are the following:

Baseball is indeed very popular in Cuba.

Fidel Castro is a fan of the game.

Numerous Cuban ballplayers of late have become stars in Major League Baseball.

Castro did attend the University of Havana and is known to have at some point traveled to the Dominican Republic, yet another Central American bastion of baseball proficiency and fanaticism.

And that's about it. . . .

A historian with an interest in both Cuba and baseball examined the newspaper records of the pertinent time period (given the fact that Havana was a significant newspaper town, with no fewer than six major papers and a dozen minor ones in regular circulation), and despite extensive coverage of baseball at both the university and local levels, there is nary a mention of Fidel.

Not on a roster.

Not in a picture.

Not even a throwaway line in a background article on rising baseball stars.

To think that a major U.S. team would bother to scout a player who had not already attracted local attention is dubious at best.

Yale professor Roberto González Echevarría did find a single mention of minor interest: "I found the box score of an intramural game played between the Law and the Business Schools at the University of Havana where a certain F. Castro pitched and lost, 5–4, in late November 1946; this is likely to be the only published box score in which the future dictator appears" (*El Mundo,* November 28, 1946).

An intramural game? Not exactly the place one would be looking for a star player, even less likely given that it was between the law school and the business school, tantamount to booking a phone booth for the reunion of MLB players who played for Harvard, Yale, and Oxford . . . and then finding out that you could sublet the remaining space for a profit.

Ergo, the awful truth is not just that Fidel was never scouted by a major American team, he was probably never scouted by anyone. Ability aside, there is no reason to suspect that he would set aside his law studies for the decadence of pro ball in Cuba, let alone in the United States.

This appears to be one of those cases of disinformation that was circulated at one point to undermine the credibility of the man with the cigar who has consistently refused to bend to the American will. To say that such a serious man might have tossed away his serious pursuits for a chance at the great American pastime is more than slightly ludicrous.

It would not have been inconsistent for the man to play for Cuba—but he didn't.

Didn't even try.

And that's fine.

Neither Bill Clinton nor George W. Bush played for their countries either.

(Buying into a team as an owner doesn't count, especially when your investment did not include your own hard-earned money! With this I am sure Fidel would agree.)

The Great Escape was really not so great

O ne of the most memorable noncombat incidences of World War II was the 1944 mass escape from Stalag Luft III, which inspired the film *The Great Escape* (based on the book of the same name by Paul Brickhill). Allied POWs valiantly planned and executed a daring mass escape of eighty-seven to bedevil and distract the Gestapo all across Axis-held territory.

Filled with details on the simultaneous excavation of three tunnels (Tom, Dick, and Harry, respectively), the master plan of distraction, deception, and preparation was perpetrated by the prisoners under the noses of the Nazis. Also nail-biting were the actual night of the escape and the escapees' subsequent paths of flight, including the memorable Hilts "The Cooler King," as played by Steve McQueen, trying to leap a barbed-wire barricade on a motorcycle (à la Evel Knievel). This so-called "Great Escape" has become a permanent fixture of World War II pop culture both on the silver screen and in subsequent parody form on such TV programs as *Get Smart* (in an episode titled "The Not So Great Escape"), *The Simpsons* (in an episode titled "A Streetcar Named Marge," which featured a subplot of baby Maggie engineering a similar maneuver at the Ayn Rand Daycare facility), and in the movie *Chicken Run*, to name just a few.

But the awful truth of the matter is that the so-called Great Escape was simply not that great.

The plot as conceived was indeed audacious. It was engineered by master escape artist of the RAF Roger Bushell (codename X), who had escaped from German custody several times only to be repeatedly recaptured before achieving the sanctuary of Allied or neutral territory. He had been shot down in 1940 and been on the run or in custody ever since then, including the time when he was in hiding in Prague, only to be caught by a dragnet that had been set up to apprehend the assassins of the Nazi Reinhardt Heydrich and not just another RAF POW on the run. After his numerous solo attempts Bushell knew that only a well-thought-out escape effort done on a massive scale would ensure any chance of real success.

Success was indeed important to Bushell; his captors had warned him that should he be recaptured again, he very well might be executed.

Bushell's plan was simple.

The entire camp would be mobilized for a single mass escape effort.

Teams were set up to act as diversions, obtain and hide supplies, forge papers and manufacture disguises, and, most important, excavate not one but three different tunnels simultaneously to facilitate the flight of 250 POWs who would then bedevil the Nazi war effort, if not by making it back to England and rejoining the Allied Forces, then by distracting the Axis war effort by tying up the various SS and Gestapo forces that would be sent to track them down.

The plan was indeed ingenious, and everyone pitched in to make it work.

Over the next year and a half surreptitious plans were made for the dispersal of the tunnel dirt in a manner the Nazis would not recognize. The inmates resorted to bribery and thievery to track down necessary documents, schedules, and maps to facilitate the escapees once they reached the other side of the warning wire and were on the run.

And despite a few setbacks (including the discovery and forced dismantlement of one of the tunnels and the abandonment of one of the others), work progressed until zero hour on March 24, 1944, when the escape was launched with the immediate discovery of an error.

The tunnel was too short and did not reach the safety of the tree line, thus resulting in a much slower escape to freedom. The exodus continued until around five A.M., when the tunnel was discovered in the early morning light.

The Great Escape was now over . . . but exactly how great was it in terms of its effectiveness and the accomplishment of its goals?

Well, in rough summation:

- Of the targeted goal of getting 250 men across the wire, only 87 made it that far.

- Of the 87 who made it across the wire, only 76 made it outside of the vicinity of the camp.

- Of the targeted goal of tying up the German forces all over Germany (particularly the SS and the Gestapo) with the task of apprehending the massive number of escapees, most of them were caught in the immediate area surrounding Sagan, the location of the nearest train station from whence the escapees were supposed to make connections and spread out in all directions.

- Of the targeted goal of distracting the Germans for a prolonged period of time, the vast majority (over 75 percent) of the escapees were apprehended within ten days of the escape.

As to other denigrating factors of the operation, one must also remember that only three prisoners actually made it to Allied or neutral territory, while fifty, more than half of the number to make it out of the camp (including Roger Bushell) were executed almost immediately upon recapture.

It is also worth noting that this was not the only "sensational" escape from this camp. Another attempt was immortalized in *The Wooden Horse* by Eric Williams, in which a pair of escapees used a wooden vaulting horse to get closer to the wire, thereby shortening the distance they needed to tunnel . . . and as other prisoners did vaulting exercises above, they dug their way to freedom below.

With regard to such matters as the number of Americans involved in the actual escape, the answer is only one: a southerner who had joined the RAF in Canada, and was therefore down in the military records as being Canadian. All of the other Americans had been transferred to a different section of the camp six months prior to zero hour and were therefore unable to access the escape tunnels once they were completed. It is also noteworthy that once the plan to relocate the American prisoners was discovered, the tunnel work was accelerated in hopes of finishing before those transfers took place; this resulted in a certain amount of slipshod security, the outcome of which was the Nazis' discovery and shutdown of the tunnel, thus further delaying the overall execution of the plan.

As for Hilts's daring motorcycle escape attempt—it didn't happen.

Hilts was probably based on an RAF prisoner named Barry Mahon, who had earned the nickname of The Cooler King through his numerous escape attempts . . . but he never participated in a motorcycle chase. (That was strictly Hollywood embellishment.) He did, however, serve as a technical adviser on the film.

The Awful Truth

is

That These Famous
Science Fiction Authors

Andre Norton
C. L. Moore

&

James Tiptree, Jr.

Were All Women

DiMaggio: Not as humble as we thought

When it comes to the legendary Yankee Clipper, there are several facts that are not in dispute.

Joe DiMaggio is the only athlete in North American professional sports history to be on four championship teams in his first four full seasons. In total, he led the Yankees to nine titles in thirteen years.

Joe DiMaggio became the first baseball player to sign for $100,000 (a $70,000 contract plus bonuses).

Over the course of his career he amassed 361 home runs, averaged 118 runs batted in (RBI) annually, compiled a .325 lifetime batting average, and struck out only 369 times. He won two batting crowns and three MVP awards.

His fifty-six-game hitting streak (May 15 to July 16, 1941) is considered by many to be the top baseball feat of all time.

His marriage to Marilyn Monroe made him fodder for the gossip pages, while his exploits in Yankee Stadium made him a sports legend.

He was "Joltin' Joe" and the "Yankee Clipper" and the subject of songs written by such diverse composers as Richard Rodgers and Oscar Hammerstein, Les Brown, Woody Guthrie, and Paul Simon and Art Garfunkel.

What is also not in dispute is how he was to be introduced after his retirement: "Joe DiMaggio, Baseball's Greatest Living Ballplayer."

Why?

Because he demanded it in his contract.

Because the awful truth is that no matter how good DiMaggio was as a ballplayer, he was even better at looking out for his own interests.

It was not enough that he be treated right, he had to be treated better than anyone else.

The title Baseball's Greatest Living Ballplayer says it all. It is not limited to a time or a place or a position in the game. It's absolute definitiveness says that, no matter who you are, Joe D. is a better baseball player than you . . . and that includes Willie Mays, Hank Aaron, Ted Williams, and anyone else who might have the stats to contest it.

Joe D. was also one of the first professional athletes to realize the financial value of one's name and reputation well after one's actual sport's career ended. Whether he was shilling for the Bowery Savings Bank or Mr. Coffee, speaking on the rubber chicken circuit, or signing memorabilia for an agreed upon fee, Joe knew how to make money off his reputation . . . and in all of the cases, Joe approved the rules before he showed up.

Baseball's Greatest Living Ballplayer played by his *own* rules, and if you wanted to play, you had to follow them and pay up front.

But money wasn't the only thing he demanded—he also demanded respect.

Richard Ben Cramer in his biography *Joe DiMaggio: The Hero's Life* relates a very telling tale in his introduction.

DiMaggio was chagrined about having to show up for the dedication of the newest monument in Yankee Stadium in 1995 (the team stars from the past were obligated to make an appearance as a sort of honor guard for such occasions). Mickey Mantle had passed away and was being feted with an honor befitting his status as one of the greatest Yankees of all time.

Allegedly, Joe didn't see what the big deal was, and he didn't understand why he had to show the Mick any last token of respect. *(After all, what did the Mick ever do for me?)*

The imposition on his time, though, turned out to be only a minor matter compared to the bigger affront to his ego.

Rawlings had issued a special game-ready Mickey Mantle commemorative ball, officially authorized by Major League Baseball for the occasion, and the balls were currently selling on the collector's market at a premium price, which equaled twice as much as a ball signed by DiMaggio himself.

Joe made sure that this slight was set right; as a result, September 27, 1998, was declared Joe DiMaggio Day in New York City. As part of the celebration at Yankee Stadium, Rawlings issued a special regulation game-ready DiMaggio ball. In return for Rawlings's use of his name, Joe D. demanded and received fifteen thousand free balls for his own personal use. His own balls were the only ones he would sign, thus assuring himself (and his company Yankee Clipper Enterprises) of being able to sell a true collectible on an exclusive basis at a price he himself would determine.

Take that, Mickey Mantle!

Mickey Mantle lived like there was no tomorrow . . . because he believed there wasn't for him

When Joe DiMaggio retired in 1952, he was replaced in center field by a switch hitter who had previously played both third base and right field. In no time at all the Yankee Clipper (soon to be called Baseball's Greatest Living Ballplayer) was replaced in the hearts and minds of Yankee fans as well.

This replacement's name was Mickey Mantle, and he went on to play for the Yankees for the rest of his career in Major League Baseball. In 2,290 games he made only 107 errors.

In 1956 Mantle won the National League Triple Crown, leading the majors with a .353 batting average, 52 home runs, and 130 runs batted in (RBIs) on the way to his first of three MVP awards. (Though the American League Triple Crown has been won twice since then, Mantle remains the last man to win the Major League Triple Crown.) On January 16, 1961, he became the highest-paid baseball player by signing a $75,000 contract ($5,000 more than DiMaggio, exclusive of bonuses).

Though many remember him for his home run race with Roger Maris in pursuit of Babe Ruth's record of sixty home runs in a single season, his other career accomplishments include the World Series records for home runs (eighteen), runs scored (forty-two), and RBIs (forty). So it was no wonder that as soon as he was eligible for consideration for the Baseball Hall of Fame, in 1974 he was voted in (DiMaggio didn't make it in until his third year of eligibility).

The man was everything you could want in a ballplayer, and he was determined to live life like there was no tomorrow . . .

. . . because the awful truth of the matter was that he actually believed that there *was* no tomorrow.

Mantle's father had died at forty from Hodgkin's disease, and he had several uncles who all died before even reaching age forty.

The Mick was constantly confronted with his own mortality. He suffered from osteomyelitis (an acute and painful bone condition), which was subject to painful flare-ups and related complications from other injuries for the rest of his life (the condition resulted in his being exempted from military service). He embraced the football adage that "you have to play hurt," and if he was well enough to play ball, he was also well enough to enjoy his off hours . . . which he did with a gusto unmatched by other players of his caliber at the time, perhaps even rivaling the revelries of the legendary Babe Ruth himself.

A hangover was nothing compared with the day-to-day pain he normally felt.

He was a regular at Toot's Shor's restaurant and all the other jock bars around town with his drinking buddy Billy Martin (after whom he named his son) even on the night before a big game.

(It should be noted that Billy Martin died in a car accident, allegedly coming home from a bar, and Billy Mantle, like son like father, died of a heart attack while in rehab/detox at the age of twenty-six).

And an additional awful truth is that Mantle's greatest fear proved to be wrong.

He didn't die young of some congenital form of cancer.

What killed him was the wear and tear the years of over-indulgence had wrought on his body.

A forty-six-year-old Mantle purportedly said, "If I knew I was going to live this long, I would have taken better care of myself."

On June 8, 1994, Mantle received a liver transplant after his had been damaged by years of chronic alcoholism, cirrhosis, and hepatitis C. Reportedly he was at that time finally on the wagon and fully rehabbed . . . but it was too late. He died on August 13, 1995, in Dallas, Texas, at Baylor University Medical Center, the cancer having already spread throughout his body.

He was almost sixty-four.

He lived close to twenty-five years longer than he thought he would, but far shorter than he might have had he practiced a bit of restraint.

Senator Joseph McCarthy had nothing to do with the Hollywood blacklist

The House Un-American Activities Committee (HUAC), which was deemed by many eventually to be responsible for the so-called Hollywood blacklist, grew from a special investigating committee established in May 1938. The committee was chaired by Martin Dies and cochaired by Samuel Dickstein, and it was initially known as the Dies Committee. Its work was supposed to be aimed mostly at German American involvement in Nazi and Ku Klux Klan activity. This inquiry was eventually dropped and their interest turned to Communist infiltration specifically in the area of the arts, starting with the Federal Theater Project in late 1938.

The committee came into prominence after World War II when it acted on suspicions that some Communist sympathizers worked within the U.S. government and various institutions of influence in American society (specifically those linked to Marxist groups and the "Popular Front" during the run up to the war). Individuals such as W. E. B. DuBois and I. F. Stone were found to have been affiliated with literally dozens of suspect groups (though, in reality, many of the groups were nothing more than glorified petition drives and "do-gooder groups" that disappeared after a single publicity campaign on behalf of a particular cause).

What the committee maintained was that such groups, acting as fronts for foreign interests at odds with the American cause, could disseminate propaganda and influence elections. In October 1947, a list of suspected Communists, deemed "subversives," working in the Hollywood film industry were summoned to appear before the House Un-American Activities Committee. Ten of them refused to give evidence, citing their First Amendment rights.

These ten were Alvah Bessie (screenwriter), Herbert Biberman (screenwriter/director), Lester Cole (screenwriter), Edward Dmytryk (director), Ring Lardner, Jr. (screenwriter), John Howard Lawson (screenwriter), Albert Maltz (screenwriter), Samuel Ornitz (screenwriter), Adrian Scott (screenwriter/film producer), and Dalton Trumbo (screenwriter).

The United States House of Representatives of the Eightieth Congress voted 346 to 17 on that November 24 to approve citations for contempt of Congress. These men, soon dubbed the "Hollywood Ten," were convicted in 1948. Following unsuccessful appeals and denial of review by the Supreme Court, they all served prison terms ranging from six months to a year. Specifically, they were in part cited for contempt for their disdain for the proceedings, and they were considered by some as being disruptive of the committee's proceedings by making political statements while refusing to answer certain questions put to them concerning their alleged Communist affiliations and activities. The famous questions "Are you a member of the Screen Writers Guild?" and "Are you now or have you ever been a member of the Communist Party?" have entered an infamous part of American oral history and are often held up to ridicule and parody. Their defense was based on the First Amendment: "Congress shall make no law respecting an establishment of religion, or prohibiting the free exercise thereof; or abridging the freedom of speech, or of the press; or the right of the people peaceably to assemble, and to petition the Government for a redress of grievances." (The committee's charges against the Hollywood Ten were problematic since being a member of the American Communist Party was not a crime in and of itself; indeed, other witnesses were not charged after claiming the right to refuse to answer in accordance with the Fifth Amendment: "No person shall be held to answer for a capital, or otherwise infamous crime, unless on a presentment or indictment of a Grand Jury, except in cases arising in the land or naval forces, or in the Militia, when in actual service in time of

War or public danger; nor shall any person be subject for the same offence to be twice put in jeopardy of life or limb; nor shall be compelled in any criminal case to be a witness against himself, nor be deprived of life, liberty, or property, without due process of law; nor shall private property be taken for public use, without just compensation.")

In response to pressure, on November 17, 1947, the Screen Actors Guild (SAG) voted to make its officers take a non-Communist pledge. Their statement declared the Hollywood Ten would be fired and not rehired until they were acquitted or purged of contempt and *had sworn that they were not Communists*. Because of their notoriety, they were unable to obtain work in the American film and television industry for many years. Subsequent blacklisting beyond this initial ten did not always involve further congressional involvement. It was often handled at the studio and union levels and influenced by nonpolitical matters.

This was undoubtedly a shameful incident in American history . . . but it had nothing to do with Senator Joseph McCarthy. The HUAC was established well before McCarthy was elected to the federal office. What's more, it was a House committee and had no connection with McCarthy, who served in the Senate.

Joseph McCarthy was a Wisconsin farm-bred boy of German and Irish descent who, after questionably auspicious service in the military during World War II (depending on whose sources you believe), ran for the Senate and in 1946 took his place in Washington as the then junior senator from Wisconsin.

He was your typical quiet backbencher until in a Lincoln Day speech of February 9, 1950 (given to the Republican Women's Club of Wheeling, West Virginia), he decreed something along the lines of "I have here in my hand a list of two hundred and five people who were known to the secretary of state as being members of the Communist Party, and who, nevertheless, are still working and shaping the policy of the State Department." (Please note that this was two years after the Hollywood blacklist resolution by the SAG.)

McCarthy parlayed this notoriety through his party's support against the Truman administration to plum power positions in the Senate, eventually snagging himself a spot as chairman of the Senate Permanent Subcommittee on Investigations. However, unlike most partisan witch-hunters, Senator McCarthy continued his take-no-prisoners anti-Communist jihad against suspected Communists in the government even after the Republicans had secured the executive branch with the election of Dwight D. Eisenhower. Eventually he lost support even within his own party.

Whether Joseph McCarthy was really an ideologically driven "Red hater" or just a publicity hound who latched onto the issue that he thought would keep him in the limelight is subject to debate.

The fact that the word *McCarthyism* was originally coined specifically to describe the anti-Communist/anti-Red movement that existed in America in the 1950s—and has now become generalized to include any government activity that seeks to suppress unfavorable political or social views, often through limiting or suspending civil rights under the pretext of maintaining national security—only further illustrates the amount of spleen felt against the man.

But though he may have been guilty of having no decency (as uttered by Joseph Welch in the televised McCarthy hearings, with the now famous sound bite "Have you no sense of decency, sir? At long last, have you left no sense of decency?") and of being an opportunist or at best a narrow-minded anti-Communist paranoid zealot, the awful truth of the matter is that he had nothing to do with the Hollywood blacklist.

(The author wishes to acknowledge his enlightenment on this issue through the works and pronouncements of Ms. Ann Coulter; even a broken clock—nondigital of course—tells the correct time twice a day.)

Okay, Roy, I'll leave Hollywood off the list, but
I still don't know what you see in that Judy Garland…

Roy Cohn, Joe McCarthy's right-hand man, was gay

Roy Cohn was the epitome of contradictions. A ruthless and ambitious attorney who was the right-hand man of the infamous Senator Joseph McCarthy on his crusade against Communism and in the name of national security, he later became a legal hired gun in the name of personal profit, even if his clients ran counter to the aforementioned national security. He was also a self-loathing Jew who was known to indulge in anti-Semitic rants, and a homosexual who openly advocated against gays.

After a top-notch education in the best schools New York had to offer, and with a degree from Columbia Law School, Roy Marcus Cohn established himself as a heavy hitter in the U.S. Attorney's office in Manhattan. He accomplished this through his prominent role in the trial of eleven leaders of the American Communist Party and in the successful 1951 prosecution of Julius Rosenberg and Ethel Rosenberg for the capital offense of selling the secrets of the atomic bomb to the Russians.

These events brought him to the attention of the legendary head of the FBI, J. Edgar Hoover, who admired Cohn's staunch anti-Communist beliefs and his "by any means necessary" drive in pursuit of justice.

Hoover in turn recommended him to then senator Joseph McCarthy for his open position as chief counsel for the Senate Investigative Committee, which McCarthy headed.

Cohn rose to the occasion, bringing his bulldog tactics of

grand-jury interrogation to the old-boy cordiality of Senate committee sessions.

With the young New York lawyer at his side, McCarthy managed a Red-baiting jihad against all of his political enemies in the name of national security. Cohn was ruthless and thorough in supporting the senator's arguments—often holding witnesses to the highest standards of oversight through continuous adversarial interrogation, and often calling their character, loyalty, and integrity into question.

These tactics proved quite successful until a matter from Cohn's own closet was used against him.

Cohn had arranged for a longtime friend, G. David Schine, to be given leave from the army to serve on McCarthy's subcommittee as an unpaid consultant. Schine's only qualifications seem to have been that he had written an eight-page booklet called "Definition of Communism," which he placed in the hotels his family owned, and his close personal relationship to Cohn. When Schine was actually drafted and close to being sent to Korea, Cohn relentlessly attempted to get him an official assignment on the committee. When negotiating with the army failed, Cohn tried bullying and intimidation through the powers of the senate committee itself.

These tactics backfired in public, however, when the army began to fight fire with fire, subtly exposing the real motivations behind Cohn's manipulations.

At one point, Joseph Welch, the army's attorney, asked McCarthy about a doctored photo (of Secretary Stevens smiling at Schine) that was being used to impeach his previous testimony before the committee:

Welch: Did you think this [photo] came from a pixie? . . .
McCarthy: Will the counsel for my benefit define—I think he might be an expert on that—what a pixie is?
Welch: Yes, I should say, Senator, that a pixie is a close relative of a fairy. Shall I proceed, sir? Have I enlightened you?

The room erupted into laughter, Cohn hardly able to contain his pique and embarrassment. This, coupled with Welch's famous rebuke: "Have you no sense of decency, sir? At long last, have you left no sense of decency?" (both exchanges were caught on camera for the public's later viewing), were the straws that broke the camel's back, and led to the political castration of the McCarthy–Cohn Red-hunting juggernaut. Before the end of the year, both men had had their era of influence and fear greatly curtailed.

McCarthy was censured and Roy Cohn forced to resign from his congressional work. Cohn then took a position with a prestigious New York law firm that allowed him to continue influence peddling among the right-wing elite (including Red-baiting fellow travelers like Richard M. Nixon and Ronald Reagan), while representing numerous New York luminaries, including Donald Trump, the Mafia, and even the New York archdiocese of the Catholic Church on different sorts of legal and governmental matters.

Just because he no longer had a position in the government did not mean that Cohn couldn't wield governmental influence. In his words, "My idea of real power is not people who hold office. They're here today and gone tomorrow. Power means the ability to get things done. It stems from friendship in my case."

Or, perhaps more precisely, in his case, "friendship and fear."

Though Cohn's sexuality was far from unusual at the time, it was an extreme contradiction to his public life in right-wing politics. He often targeted government officials and cultural figures not only for Communist sympathies but for alleged homosexual tendencies, which might compromise their security clearance. It was also rumored that he sometimes used sexual secrets and/or rumors as blackmail tools to gain informants or pressure witnesses to testify and/or corroborate other testimony that might have been seminal to his allegations. In the post-Stonewall era of gay liberation, Cohn was said to frequent gay bars on both coasts (and in Key West) semi-openly, but he still denied all rumors, refusing to leave the closet. He continued to lend his support to antigay political campaigns, and during the debate over New York City's first gay rights law, he advocated that homosexuals shouldn't be allowed to be schoolteachers. While privately battling his own rampant AIDS infection, he publicly attested that he was in fact suffering from liver cancer, lest anyone believe he actually might be gay.

Though always a man in desire of the public eye, Cohn probably would not be comfortable with the posthumous iconic stature that has been afforded him as a character in Tony Kushner's award-winning play *Angels in America*, which portrayed him warts, gay proclivities, and all, in fictional scenes that mirrored his actual AIDS-caused death.

Rather than as an icon of the right, he will instead be remembered as an enigmatic figure, closeted and self-loathing.

The Mertzes hated each other

If Lucy and Ricky Ricardo of *I Love Lucy* fame are considered the first family of television situation comedies, then undoubtedly Fred and Ethel Mertz are the first family of television situation comedy sidekicks.

Whether as foils or as coconspirators in Lucy's zany plots, Fred and Ethel provided a perfect balance to the show that, nonetheless, failed to steal the spotlight from TV's first female superstar. Where Lucy and Ricky were the show-biz yuppies on the rise, Fred and Ethel were the everymen, slightly dowdy, and not the least bit high society (despite the fact that Fred also had show-biz roots in vaudeville and was evidently successful enough to be able to afford to own a Manhattan apartment house).

Fred was the grouchy, skinflint curmudgeon with a heart of gold.

Ethel was the small-town girl he married who always needed to lose a few pounds and longed for a life in which every penny wasn't prepinched.

They were the experienced older couple always willing to provide the younger Ricardos with a helping hand, a bit of guile, and an occasional complaint or two.

As the Ricardos were a show-biz match made in heaven, the Mertzes were a match made on Earth. Maybe things weren't heavenly, but they were definitely stable and content, with lots of chemistry and camaraderie.

And who but William Frawley and Vivian Vance could have played those parts?

The casting was kismet.

But the awful truth is that behind the scenes, things were far from friendly, and the chemistry onscreen dramatically concealed the chemistry offscreen, which was more akin to oil and water—they just didn't mix.

In fact, Frawley and Vance simply loathed each other.

To begin with, Frawley and Vance were not the first choices for the part. (The roles were originally conceived for Gale Gordon [who later played Mr. Mooney on *The Lucy Show*] and Bea Benaderet [who later played Kate on *Petticoat Junction* and is probably most famous as the original voice of Betty Rubble on *The Flintstones*], but contractual commitments precluded them from signing on.) Vance saw the show as an opportunity to build her career after several successful stage parts, and she threw herself into the part working with Lucy, who, despite the difference in age of their characters, was really her contemporary. Vance strove to improve each performance and innovate along the way, thus making a better show.

Frawley, on the other hand, who had many bit parts in his résumé and was twenty-five years Vance's senior, saw his part as just a paycheck, and he resented any additional work beyond showing up and doing his lines as they were written in the script. Innovation and improvisation just slowed things down and thus kept him away from the bar, the track, or another of his indulgences.

Though the TV audience had no trouble accepting their marriage, the age disparity between them irked Vance, who was once overheard by Frawley saying that he should be playing her father instead of her husband.

She was even overheard to say, "Whenever I received a new script, I raced through it, praying that there wouldn't be a scene where we had to be in bed together."

Frawley, on the other hand, was heard to respond at a later date, "She's one of the finest gals to come out of Kansas, but I often wish she'd go back there."

(These quotes were carefully kept out of the press so as to not ruin the illusion of the cast of the show as the happy little family. Moreover, it was in both stars' interest to keep it civil in the public eye; it was in each of their contracts that the dismissal of one would result in the writing out of the other.)

Vance's Emmy win in the Best Supporting Actress category in 1954 only deepened the divide between the two performers, because Frawley viewed himself as the seasoned veteran forced to perform alongside a lesser talent.

One of the continuing themes of the show was that Lucy was the only one in the group who seemed to be incapable of succeeding in show business. Fred's experience in vaudeville provided an excuse for him and Ethel to perform together occasionally in some of Ricky's shows, which usually resulted in Frawley and Vance sharing a duet or two. On one occasion, Frawley derided Vance for trying to tell him how to do a simple soft-shoe number, declaring, "I've been in vaudeville since I was five years old," and will "probably end up teaching old fat-ass [Vance]."

Vance responded later, "I loathed William Frawley and the feeling was mutual."

Desi Arnaz (Ricky) was also the producer of the show, and he was always looking for another way to make a fast buck. So when the decision was made to cut back slightly on the show's output (coinciding with the Ricardos' move to Connecticut in the *I Love Lucy* time line), he broached the idea of producing a spin-off show focusing on just the Mertzes. The money people were quite enthused and were convinced it would be a surefire hit; thus, they were willing to bankroll substantial raises for both Frawley and Vance.

Frawley was as enthused as he ever got; the idea of more money for about the same amount of work appealed to him (not to mention the security of a continuing paycheck once *I Love Lucy* had come to an end, which he saw as the eventual outcome of the show's winding down).

Vance, on the other hand, would have none of it. She fulfilled the rest of her contract but vowed never to work with Frawley again, no matter how much money they threw at her . . . and so, because of this personal animosity, the potentially blockbuster spin-off never occurred.

Soon thereafter, *I Love Lucy* folded production.

William Frawley went on to the role of Bub in the early years of another successful sitcom, *My Three Sons*, while Vance landed a leading role in the sitcom *Guestward Ho*, which quickly failed to secure an audience and was canceled.

Eventually she reteamed with Lucy on *The Lucy Show* in the character of Vivian, a younger, not quite as dowdy version of Ethel Mertz.

The Awful Truth

is
That
Men's Fiction Authors

Jack Cannon *(author of the Joe Ryker series)*

Simon Quinn *(author of the Inquisitor series)*

&

John Lange *(author of Odds On and Easy Go)*

Are Actually
Bestselling Authors

Nelson DeMille
Martin Cruz Smith

&

Michael Crichton

The father and daughter of *Father Knows Best* didn't know best

Father Knows Best* began on the radio (under the less definitive title *Father Knows Best?*) and moved to TV on October 3, 1954, where it aired a total of 203 episodes, through September 17, 1962. The show eventually appeared on all three of the television networks of the time, an amazing feat in television history.

The show portrayed a certain idealization of white, middle-class American life, with messages ranging from "lies are not helpful" to "everyone can have a bad day" to "the American way of life is much better than the life of tyranny under a Communist rule." Messages aside, it was the perfect Norman Rockwell portrait of the good and true American family, and nowhere was this more apparent than in the relationship between the father, Jim Anderson, and the youngest daughter, Kathy "Kitten" Anderson. He was the strong, supportive, good-natured father, always ready to dispense a humorous pick-me-up or some well-thought-out advice and guidance. She was the precocious, yet naïve, playful trickster who was still sheltered from the evils of the world that existed beyond the confines of the TV studio "household" setting. The actors playing these parts, Robert Young and Lauren Chapin, were well received by their audience and earned accolades for their performances (two Emmys for Young and five Milky Ways—an award for youthful performers—for Chapin).

Playing the archetypal father and daughter was proof positive of their acting abilities because their offscreen lives were quite another story.

Robert Young, who was also one of the show's creators, was prone to major bouts of depression and had a tendency toward alcoholism, and as the series went on he began to feel more and more restrained by the confines of this role, with which he was now universally associated. While the camera was rolling, he was fine; when it wasn't, he withdrew and became distant, cutting himself off from his TV family under the dark cloud of depression.

Far from the happy daddy of the show, Young was the troubled modern man who felt like a hamster on a wheel—no progress, just day after day of wearing fatigue.

Chapin, who was no longer a child when the show stopped production, had an even tougher time. Her home life had always been a mess, with instances of emotional and physical abuse rampant and a family history of alcoholism. She was looked upon as the family's meal ticket yet denied any personal affirmation of her own worth. Though adored as Kitten on TV, her own mother saw fit to tell her that she would never be beautiful or even pretty.

Thus, once the run of the show was over, Lauren was in a quandary, and prone to making bad choices . . . not just bad career choices like appearing in less than savory productions such as *The Amorous Adventures of Don Quixote and Sancho Panza* (also known as *The Erotic Adventures of Don Quixote* and *When Sex Was a Knightly Affair*), but really bad life choices such as numerous abusive boyfriends, narcotics, and promiscuity.

After her first bad marriage and a miscarriage, Chapin hooked up with a boyfriend who introduced her to heroin and convinced her that her acting skills could still be quite lucrative, especially if she took her "little girl" performance to clients who liked that sort of thing and were more than willing to pay for it. TV's "Kitten" could be a "Pussycat" for hire. Out of misguided love and memories of her upbringing (where her acting was little more than prostitution to bring money home for an ungrateful family), Lauren accepted his guidance and began turning tricks in no time.

Her next few years were filled with heartbreak, medical problems, arrests, suicide attempts, prison and sanitarium stays, as she continued a downward spiral to a world never alluded to in *Father Knows Best*. Only after an intervention by her son and a strong and loving support group (and, according to her memoir, the grace of God) was she able to turn her life around and abandon the depravity of an existence that ranked among the most depressing of those covered by *E! True Hollywood Story* and *Hollywood Babylon*.

Though cynics today find it hard to swallow the idealism of the shows that came out of the 1950s, claiming that the world then must have been a very naïve place, even they would shudder at the darkness that lay within everyone's favorite father and daughter.

John Wayne never served in the armed forces

O nscreen, his military career has been all encompassing and inspiring.

He covered all forces in the service.

The Army:
Back to Bataan
Island in the Sky
The Longest Day
Cast a Giant Shadow
The Green Berets

The Air Force:
Flying Tigers
Jet Pilot

The Cavalry:
Rio Grande
She Wore a Yellow Ribbon
Fort Apache

The Coast Guard:
The Sea Spoilers

The Marines:
Without Reservations
Sands of Iwo Jima
The Flying Leathernecks

The Navy:
Salute
Seven Sinners
Fighting Seabees
They Were Expendable
The Wings of Eagles
In Harm's Way
Operation Pacific

The Texas Volunteers:
The Alamo

The Union Army:
The Undefeated
How the West Was Won
The Horse Soldiers

He also played his fair share of famous leaders in military history:

> *How the West Was Won* (1962) . . . General William Tecumseh Sherman
> *The Longest Day* (1962) . . . Lieutenant Colonel Benjamin Vandervoort
> *The Alamo* (1960) . . . Colonel Davy Crockett
> *The Conqueror* (1956) . . . Temujin, later known as Genghis Khan
> *The Greatest Story Ever Told* (1965) . . . Centurion at the Crucifixion, a short but significant stint as a soldier in Caesar's army

John Wayne was definitely the poster boy for the armed services and the archetype of both the exemplary American military leader and the rank-and-file GI. This was a very neat accomplishment given the fact that he never actually served in the military.

This is not to say that he was a draft dodger or a 4F or even a pacifist. His stage name John Wayne is alleged to have been inspired by the memory of Revolutionary War hero and patriot officer "Mad Anthony" Wayne . . . but nonetheless in terms of a service record, his is nonexistent.

There is evidence to suggest that he applied to and was turned down by Annapolis Naval Academy for unknown reasons. According to an interview with the Duke, "More than anything else, I wanted to go to Annapolis and become an officer in the navy. It was a terrible disappointment when I didn't make it."

Born Marion Robert Morrison in Winterset, Iowa, in 1907 (his name was later changed to Marion Michael Morrison by his parents), the legendary Duke had obviously missed out on any combat opportunites in World War I due to his age.

The same cannot be said of World War II when, with his name changed to John Wayne and a Hollywood career neatly on track with the success of his portrayal of Johnny Ringo in *Stagecoach* in 1939, he was just as eligible for military service as such other Hollywood actors as Jimmy Stewart, Tyrone Power, and Clark Gable.

At the time of the attack on Pearl Harbor he was thirty-four years old, his career was just taking off after the usual period of "barely making ends meet." He had a family to feed, and an absence from the silver screen could indeed jeopardize his upswing to stardom. As a result, he asked for and received a deferral for family dependency, a classification 3-A. With a few more major films under his belt, his place in the Hollywood pantheon of stars would be assured.

Washington, D.C., was also quite aware of how important Hollywood was to the war effort, and the type of films that featured John Wayne epitomized the message that the war-focused administration wanted to present both to its citizens and the world at large.

Wayne also took part in USO tours. The iconic fighting man of the silver screen entertained the real GI Joes who were battling it out in the trenches. He also had numerous conversations with his friend, director John Ford, who was heroically engaged in a pioneer naval photography unit in the Pacific, where, on numerous occasions, the filmmaker and his crew found themselves shooting film of the enemy as the enemy shot live ammunition at them; Wayne requested paperwork to qualify for this asssignment but never followed through.

In 1943, when most 3-As were called up, the Duke requested that his classification be changed to a 2-A (deferment in the national interest), and it was.

As a result, he never served.

Partly due to his role in the making of *The Green Berets* (produced in close collaboration with the armed forces) and his jingoistic remarks on the U.S. role in Vietnam, the Duke was erroneously labeled by his antiwar detractors as a draft dodger and a 4-F (physically unfit for service).

The 4-F remark probably had its roots in his college years, perhaps in relation to his Annapolis application or his short-lived athletic career in college, where, for a short time, he played on the USC football team under legendary coach Howard Jones, only to have his athletic career curtailed by an injury incurred while supposedly swimming at the local beach. The two incidents were unrelated, and he never received a designation of 4-F.

The draft dodger remark is also more than slightly unfair.

He made his necessary appearances before the draft board, and indeed he continued to serve the national interest in what was determined to be an important role. The fact that he personally profited from that role is beside the point.

Still, the awful truth is that he never served in the armed forces.

It is also ironic that his last public appearance at the Academy Awards was to announce the winner of the Best Picture Oscar in 1978, when most of the major awards went to two decidedly antiwar films: *The Deer Hunter* and *Coming Home*.

...and after that the swagger just came naturally.
It's less noticeable when I'm on a horse.

The "silent partners" at the Academy Awards

In various award categories for the Motion Pictures Association, it is not unusual for multiple individuals to share a single nomination in a given category. Certain areas of motion-picture expertise seem always to lend themselves to collaboration, such as Art Design, Special Effects, and Cinematography, all of which represent the efforts of a team of professionals whose work coalesces into a single vision. Likewise, screenwriters and composers often share billing on a single work with credits determined through a strict and precise set of rules of arbitration. It is not uncommon for a single screenplay to have passed through numerous hands before completion, and most songs credit a pair of collaborators (the music composer and the lyricist) if not more (e.g., Best Song winner of the "Theme from *Arthur*" credited four individuals: Burt Bacharach, Carole Bayer Sager, Christopher Cross, and Peter Allen).

The acting categories, however, have been sacrosanct—one performance, one name (and, under today's rules, one performance, one nominee, the previous exception being when Barry Fitzgerald was nominated for both Best Actor and Best Supporting Actor for the same part in *Going My Way*), and, as a result, in at least two different cases the official nomination did not represent the entire performance.

In 1956 Deborah Kerr was nominated in the Best Actress category for her performance as Anna Leonowens in the film version of the Richard Rodgers and Oscar Hammerstein musical

The King and I. Rodgers and Hammerstein had a knack for creating dramatic roles in musicals that allowed the featured performers to show off the height of their abilities with a range of emotions, exacting vocal demands, and kinetic staging and choreography. *The King and I* was a perfect example of this.

Indeed, Yul Brynner's performance as the King excelled in all three areas, securing him not just the nomination for Best Actor, but the actual award as well.

Deborah Kerr, on the other hand, was really responsible for only two-thirds of the scope of her performance (the acting and dancing); her singing numbers were actually dubbed by then twenty-one-year-old Marni Nixon, whose vocal performance was not acknowledged in the credits for the film. (Nixon also provided the singing for Kerr's role in *An Affair to Remember* later that year, a performance that did not yield either of them a nomination.)

Nixon's talent enabled Hollywood to recast major Broadway musicals with female stars whose vocal talents may not have met the roles' requirements, much to the chagrin of the thespians who had originated the parts in the stage productions. Initially Natalie Wood (who replaced Carol Lawrence, Broadway's Maria) was told that she would be doing her own singing in *West Side Story*, only later to be informed that her singing would be dubbed (as were many of the other leads in the film) . . . and, in her case, the musical numbers were performed by Marni Nixon.

Likewise, when Audrey Hepburn was cast as Eliza Doolittle (a role made famous by Julie Andrews on Broadway) in the film version of *My Fair Lady,* her singing voice was replaced by, yes, Nixon's.

It is noteworthy that neither Wood's nor Hepburn's performances earned Academy Award nominations, and some have speculated that the uncredited Marni Nixon part of the performance might have had something to do with it.

Another case of a partial-performance nominee occurred in 1973, when Linda Blair was nominated for Best Supporting Actress for the film *The Exorcist*, in which she played a satanically bedeviled young girl. The problem here was that during her most severe bouts of possession, the studio had dubbed her voice in an effort to make her seem more mature, more menacing, and more malevolent.

The studio and director William Friedkin sought out Mercedes McCambridge, veteran actress and vocal dramatist from the golden days of radio, to provide the voice of Regan's demon. In an effort to heighten the film and Blair's performance's mystique, they did not list McCambridge in the credits. She then demanded arbitration through the Screen Actors Guild (SAG), a move that ultimately resulted in her being properly credited in future releases of the film. The SAG decision did not occur until well after the Academy Awards were handed out, and, not surprisingly, Blair did not win for her partial performance.

Given the special effects options that are now available to the movie industry, it is theoretically possible to digitally dub in an entire performance. The HBO series *The Sopranos* was crafted to allow Nancy Marchand a final performance after her actual death by digitally constructing a new performance by her from bits and pieces of previous performances. How far this proccess can be taken is anybody's guess, and how the Academy will respond to it is equally up in the air.

One final Academy Award anecdote on this subject:

Julie Andrews must have felt passed over when Audrey Hepburn landed her role in *My Fair Lady*, but, as luck would have it, it allowed Andrews to take the title role in the movie *Mary Poppins,* for which she received the Best Actress award in the same category in which Hepburn had failed to secure a nomination. As a slight dig to the studio that had passed her over for the other part, she started her acceptance speech saying: "Hello! I'm Marni Nixon."

There really were female astronauts in the 1960s

One of the most popular anecdotes concerning the former first lady, now senator, Hillary Rodham Clinton, involved one of her childhood career dreams:

"When I was a very young girl, I wanted to be an astronaut, so I wrote off to this new agency called NASA and asked how a twelve-year-old girl could become an astronaut. I got an answer back, saying, 'We're not accepting women into the astronaut program.' I was somewhat comforted by my mother, who told me that my eyesight was much too bad anyway."

This incident provided the basis for a critically praised science fiction story by Pamela Sargent titled "Hillary Goes to Venus" (a companion piece to "Danny Goes to Mars," which dealt with similar aspirations by former vice president Dan Quayle) . . . and also might have been the first time that Clinton had officially been lied to by someone associated with the federal government. The awful truth of the matter is that in 1961 (when the anecdote should have taken place) there was a top-secret program as part of NASA that was indeed evaluating women astronauts.

They were known as the Mercury 13. Each was subjected to and passed the very same extreme physical and psychological tests that culled the original astronauts (Alan Shepherd, Virgil Grissom, John Glenn, etc.) from the massive number of pilot applicants. These thirteen women were Jerrie Cobb, Bernice Steadman, Janey Hart, Jerri Truhill, Rhea Woltman, Sarah Ratley, Jan Dietrich, Marion Dietrich, Myrtle Cagle, Irene Leverton, Gene Nora

Jessen, Jean Hixson, and Mary Wallace "Wally" Funk . . . and they have been largely overlooked in most histories of the space program, because the program that was to feature them, quite literally, never got off the ground.

One of the original impetuses for the women's program was a desire by some of the leaders, political and military, to explore all options and opportunities that might result in a first for the United States in the space race with the Soviet Union. Indeed, the Russians had already beaten us into outer space with *Sputnik,* as well as with such "manned accomplishments" as those by Gagarin (first man in space, first man in orbit) and Leonov (first space walk), and the U.S. team quite frankly was getting sick and tired of striving for second on every outer space exploration accomplishment.

One of the founders of this female-focused program, Dr. William Randolph Lovelace II (who headed up the Lovelace Clinic, where the original Mercury 7 screening process had taken place), had invited a female flyer friend (Jerrie Cobb) to undergo the same regimen he had established for the men, and when she passed with flying colors, he and a female associate sought out other qualified women to increase the selection pool for the Mercury 13.

It was Lovelace's contention that a more diverse selection of astronauts—male and female—would increase the amount of knowledge that could be gleaned from the planned missions of the space program (which, at the time, was solely directed toward success in flight rather than ancillary acquisition of new data). There was even the remote possibility that the female of the species might be a more adaptable/advantageous candidate for the work at hand.

Not surprisingly, many disagreed.

NASA was a boy's club.

There is the story of a highly qualified female engineer with an androgynous name who accepted a position at Cape Canaveral, only to have the job offer rescinded by her superior on the basis that the space center lacked lavatory facilities for females. Though this architectural problem was indeed true at the time, it is fairly safe to say that the floor plan design was done with the understanding that there would be no room for women on the staff of the facility.

Whether this decision was based on just plain shortsightedness (after all, it was designed by the same folks who designed military bases) or sexist prejudice is hard to say; sexism was not yet a debatable topic.

Either way, NASA had in a sense already posted the NO GIRLS ALLOWED sign in front of its clubhouse.

Nevertheless, Lovelace and his thirteen female would-be astronauts (and his support staff) continued to buck the system . . . and again and again they came up against a brick wall.

The thirteen were required to undergo further testing beyond that required of the Mercury 7 in hopes that eventually they would all be eliminated from consideration.

But this was not the case: Lovelace's first choice, Jerrie Cobb, came through all three phases with flying colors.

Eventually the NASA masters resorted to the sort of preemptive screenings that could not be bested or trained for:

- The female form would cause a new design of the interior of the capsule, which would result in undo delays.

- The female metabolism is not as consistent as male metabolism due to the intrinsic effects of the menstrual cycle, which not only caused fluctuations in biochemistry but also had been linked to periodic mental instability.

- Pursuant to the previous point, the experts also had to take into account the influence of the moon on menses, and the possibility that the astronaut's closer proximity to the lunar body could cause further fluctuations that might jeopardize the stability of the individual.

And finally:

- The death of a female astronaut might be the death of the space program in terms of public support, a risk that none of the higher-ups were willing to take.

But Lovelace countered every setback with a challenge, and he advocated that the women continue undergoing training. As a result, many of the thirteen resigned their day jobs and relocated to the facility, where they could finish the testing and begin the training.

Unfortunately, on the eve of their arrival, all of the female candidates received telegrams informing them that their services would no longer be required by NASA.

The navy would not allow them access to the facility without NASA clearance, and NASA would not provide them with clearance unless they had already passed their training regimen.

The thirteen and Lovelace appealed to Washington (one of the thirteen women was married to a member of Congress), but despite support from some of the Mercury 7, the women's program was disbanded, and the time and effort put in by the Mercury 13 was left uncompensated.

An article by Clare Boothe Luce in *Life* magazine called NASA to task for its treatment of the FLATs (First Lady Astronaut Trainees) when, once the program was stonewalled for good, the Russians beat us again by launching the first woman into outer space—Valentina Tereshkova on *Vostok* 6 on June 16, 1963.

But despite the *Life* coverage, these willing and brave female pilots and the organized discrimination that grounded their program has largely been forgotten.

Vietnam was JFK's war

I t is fairly safe to say that the Vietnam War is a controversial subject for Americans, and it would appear that there are more than enough targets for blame to go around.

Perhaps the greatest injustice was that the blame was originally focused on the returning veterans, who got lambasted by both sides, pro and con.

But as time passes everything becomes political, and Vietnam became associated with the less likable president.

For some, the war can immediately be blamed on President Lyndon B. Johnson, whose Gulf of Tonkin Resolution was approved by Congress on August 7, 1964, enabling him to escalate U.S. involvement in the war "as the President shall determine."

As a result, he became the face of the war to the American people, and in a televised address Johnson claimed that "the challenge that we face in Southeast Asia today is the same challenge that we have faced with courage and that we have met with strength in Greece and Turkey, in Berlin and Korea, in Lebanon and in Cuba."

This was soon countered with peacenik slogans such as "Hey, hey, LBJ, how many kids did you kill today?" a public-opinion nightmare that was made worse by the Defense Department's less-than-candid disclosure of casualties and troop strengths and the up-close and personal coverage of the war on all of the major news networks.

For others, the war is blamed on Johnson's successor, President Richard M. Nixon, whose whispered secret plan to win the war was actually a blatant plan to win the election. This plan wound up being a policy called "Vietnamization," the outward goal of which was to foster the South Vietnamese Army to increasingly hold its own against the North Vietnamese Army, but whose unstated goal was to lessen domestic opposition to the war in the United States by shifting the primary burden of combat to the ARVN (the Army of the Republic of Vietnam, which represented the South, despite its inclusive name).

A gross simplification of the comparison of the two presidents' involvement in the war can be summed up as "more U.S. casualties under Johnson/more U.S. bombs dropped under Nixon."

But the awful truth of the matter is that Vietnam, as far as the United States was concerned, was President John F. Kennedy's war, which would have been made much more obvious had he not been assassinated three weeks after the assassination of the President of the Republic of Vietnam, Ngo Dinh Diem.

The actual conflict in Vietnam can be traced back to Ho Chi Minh's speech on September 2, 1945, when he cited the American Declaration of Independence as a reason why the United States should support his movement for an independent Vietnam (also alluding to their allied efforts against the Japanese in the previous conflict).

The United States, however, refrained from choosing sides, and in 1954 the country was divided between the South, under Diem, and the North, under Minh. By 1957 Communist guerrilla forces penetrated the South, promoting what appeared to be a northern-backed plan of insurgency.

The South looked to the United States for support, and the States complied by sending over advisers to help suppress the guerrilla forces.

In June 1961, JFK met with Soviet premier Nikita Khrushchev in Vienna, where the Soviet leader refused to back down in discussions over several key U.S.–Soviet issues. The American president left the meeting convinced that the Russians were ready for war, if not head to head, then through surrogates in various areas of influence. This led to the conclusion that Southeast Asia would most likely be the theater for Soviet-backed forces to test America's commitment to a containment policy.

President Kennedy had already seen the failure of the Bay of Pigs invasion of Communist Cuba; the construction of the Berlin Wall, cutting off East Germany from West Germany and thus allowing for further Communist domination; and a negotiated settlement between the pro-Western government of Laos and the Pathet Lao Communist movement. Fearing that another failure on the part of the United States to stop Communist expansion would fatally damage the West's position, and, of course, mindful of his own party's perception as weak on Communism, a notion fostered by the McCarthy era of scrutiny and Red-baiting propaganda, JFK was determined to go on the offensive, and Vietnam would be the battleground for his fighting back against the Communists, all along seeing the North Vietnamese as merely surrogates for the Soviets.

Add to this Kennedy's own interest in transforming the military, not just through ballistic military parity, which he used as a campaign issue, but also through so-called "special forces," which would be perfect to test out against the guerrilla insurgents in the "brushfire" puppet war that seemed to be emerging in Vietnam.

At this point it should also be noted that even though the Kennedy regime was siding with the South, they were none too wild about President Diem, who also had slightly Communist as well as Catholic leanings. Indeed, Diem's police-state-style repression of nonsupportive factions in the South (a majority of whom were pacifist Buddhist monks) caused, in the opinions of many of the advisers, a further destabilization of the Republic forces in their opposition to the North. The instability led to his assassination, and a subsequent leadership void that U.S. forces tried to fill.

Whether Kennedy might have had second thoughts on the situation after Diem's death and "strategically withdrawn" from the theater or upped the stakes with all of the intensity of a dead ender is anyone's guess. He had previously pulled the plug on the Bay of Pigs invasion but had also faced down the Soviets during the Cuban missile crisis. The awful truth is that Kennedy got the United States there, and, thus, history will have to judge Vietnam as JFK's war.

The Awful Truth

is

That These Famous
Musicians

Burt Bacharach,
Paul Shaffer,

&

Barry Manilow

Actually Wrote
(respectively)

"The Theme from The Blob"

*(which starred Steve McQueen
and a monster made of Jell-O),*

"It's Raining Men"

*(which was recorded by the
Weather Girls)*

&

"Give Your Face Something to
Smile About"

*(which was a commercial for
Stridex)*

I am sorry, Mr. Cash, but if you don't leave,
I'm going to have to call security...

Johnny Cash never went to prison as an inmate

"Johnny Cash transcends all musical boundaries, and is one of the original outlaws."

—*Willie Nelson*

"[A brilliant chronicler of] songs of hillbilly thug life [that] go right to the heart of the American underclass."

—*Quentin Tarantino*

"I have been behind bars a few times . . . sometimes of my own volition, sometimes involuntarily. Each time, I felt the same feeling of kinship with my fellow prisoners."

"I think there's a little bit of criminal in all of us. Everybody's done something they don't want anybody to know about. Maybe that's where it comes from."

—*Johnny Cash*

There is no question that Johnny Cash is the authentic American balladeer of penal servitude, tapping into the outlaw heart and the ambiguous criminal mind with bestselling albums such as *Johnny Cash at Folsom Prison* (1968) and *Johnny Cash at San Quentin* (1969), not to mention such hit songs as "Folsom Prison Blues," and "I Walk the Line." Most notably, he voluntarily performed in several prisons in concerts for convicts, for whom he felt a great compassion, as well as taking an active role in campaigning for prison reform and taking part in various counseling programs. In the mid-1980s he recorded and toured with Waylon Jennings, Willie Nelson, and Kris Kristofferson (all of whom had had previous altercations with the law for various matters) as The Highwaymen, making two hit albums that are classics of the country-western outlaw tradition.

But with that said, there is a single fact that bears mentioning.

The awful truth is that Johnny Cash never served a day of hard time in his life and saw the inside of a prison only as an invited guest and not as an inmate. Indeed, his soulful rendering of prison life, "Folsom Prison Blues," was written after seeing the B movie *Inside the Walls of Folsom Prison* while serving as a U.S. airman in West Germany in the early 1950s.

Cash was born J. R. Cash (he later had his name legally changed to Johnny) in Kingsland, Arkansas, in 1932, the son of a poor farmer who had a severe drinking problem and was physically and emotionally abusive to his family. By age five, Cash was working in the cotton fields, experiencing a life of tragedy and hardship akin to many others in the Depression-era South.

After a stint in the armed forces, and a period during which he played music at night while selling appliances during the day, in 1955 he signed with Sun Records and started his recording career. "Folsom Prison Blues," "I Walk the Line," "Guess Things Happen That Way," and other hits quickly established Cash as a major player on both the pop and country charts, and by the mid-1960s he was one of the most popular artists in the country.

Unfortunately, success led to substance abuse, and a violent and incoherent outburst in Nashville eventually got him banned from the Grand Ole Opry in 1965, regardless of his strength as a headliner and leading man in the field of country-western music.

During this time he did have numerous run-ins with the law, some of which resulted in his being taken away in handcuffs, but these only led to partial nights' stays in holding cells or occasional "sleep it off" overnighters in a jail cell . . . both of which ended in a morning farewell with a promise to appear in court at some later date.

This is not to say that he didn't have a few close calls, given his obstreperous nature and penchant for booze and drugs. In 1965 he was busted by the narcotics squad in El Paso, Texas. Though the officers wrongly suspected that he was smuggling heroin from Mexico, they were greatly disappointed to discover that the only thing they could pin on him was illegal possession of amphetamines, which he explained he was using to get through the rigors of a very demanding tour schedule. He pled out and received a suspended sentence (whether the court officials involved in the decision were Johnny Cash fans who might have attended some of his area performances was not disclosed).

He was arrested another time during yet another late-night bout of intoxication when he wound up trespassing on private property, allegedly to pick some flowers.

This, too, resulted in a slap on the wrist.

Yet despite his essentially clean record, the man shared a tortured soul with those interred in American prisons.

The man in black would always be their kin, and they would welcome him with open arms until his waning health and eventual death prevented him from any more visits for concerts or counseling.

Richard Burton never won an Academy Award

He was considered by many to be the acting superstar of his day, a respected stage thespian who also had appeal on the big screen.

Some thought of him as the new Laurence Olivier; others as the workingman's Gielgud.

He was everything American audiences looked for in an English actor, and he wasn't even English.

He was born Richard Walter Jenkins in the village of Pontrhydyfen, Wales, near Port Talbot, and he grew up in a poor, Welsh-speaking household with many brothers and sisters. He eventually changed his name to Richard Burton, and with great effort lost his Welsh accent in favor of the Queen's English, and made a name for himself as one of John Osborne's "angry young men" (having come to critical notice in the play *Look Back in Anger*).

He was promoted to leading-man status on the silver screen in *My Cousin Rachel* opposite Olivia de Havilland, and from that point on he was an archetypal Hollywood leading man, filling the screen with consistently larger-than-life portrayals and the tabloids with tales of infidelities, adulteries, and excesses, whether concerning his five marriages (the two most turbulent being those to Elizabeth Taylor) or his prodigious consumption of alcohol.

Whether on the Broadway stage as Hamlet or as King Arthur in Alan Jay Lerner and Frederick Loewe's *Camelot* (for which he won a Tony Award for Best Actor in a Musical, despite his proclivity toward talking his way through a song, which had to be obvious to audiences in a cast that included the melodious voices of Julie Andrews and Robert Goulet) or in epic films like *The Robe* and *Cleopatra*, Burton was the classic leading man with a bit of British braggadocio and class.

He was considered, when he was at the top of his game, to be one of the best of the best.

But the awful truth of the matter is that he never actually won an Academy Award.

He was nominated seven times in the category of Best Actor for roles in the following films:

- *My Cousin Rachel*

- *The Robe*

- *Becket*

- *The Spy Who Came in from the Cold*

- *Who's Afraid of Virginia Woolf?*

- *Anne of a Thousand Days*

- *Equus*

(Four were based on successful dramatic plays, three were historical epic costume dramas, one was a surreal drama, and two were contemporary psychological thrillers—quite the broad spectrum of talented performance for any single actor.)

Yet he never won.

True, he had more than his share of cinematic embarrassments (many of which were starring opposite on-again, off-again lover/wife Taylor) including *Cleopatra, Boom,* and *Hammersmith Is Out,* as well as real bombs such as *Candy, Staircase,* and *Exorcist II: The Heretic,* all of which reeked of performing for money rather than art . . . but he also had glimmers of greatness in small parts such as his narration in the movie *Zulu* and his last big-screen appearance as O'Brien in the 1984 version of *1984.*

Over the course of his career he amassed two Golden Globes,

a British Film Academy Award, a Theater World Award, a Tony, and even a Grammy . . . but never an Oscar.

At the time of his death, he was tied with Peter O'Toole for the most number of nominations without a win.

Always a bridesmaid . . . never a bride.

Russ Meyer's award-winning film work

Russ Meyer, the so-called "King of the Nudies" and the "Father of Sexploitation," is considered to be the true pioneer of commercially viable adult filmmaking, with his 1959 landmark classic *The Immoral Mr. Teas*. It was the story of a meek voyeur who had the ability to see through women's clothing. Made on a shoestring budget, the movie went on to make a substantial profit on the stag-film circuit while pushing the limits of what could be filmed for the adult market (i.e., substantially more nudity than anyone previously thought) without eschewing the possibility of a commercial release (rather than the usual "private screenings" via stag/bachelor parties).

With titles like *Skyscrapers and Brassieres* and *Mondo Topless*, for the most part his films are more ribaldry than X-rated pornography (though they do seem unusually fixated on women with large breasts). He cowrote *Beyond the Valley of the Dolls* with Pulitzer Prize–winning film critic Roger Ebert in 1970 (one of Meyer's two major studio films; the other was *The Seven Minutes* [1971], based on the bestselling novel of the same title by Irving Wallace, which dealt with the legal issue of obscenity in a court case).

Faster, Pussycat! Kill! Kill! is usually considered to be his definitive masterpiece, or at least his most idiosyncratic, while *Beneath the Valley of the Ultravixens*, his final film proper (1979), is considered his funniest.

But despite this filmmaker's lurid profile and reputation, some of his work has been deemed worthy not only of critical praise but of no fewer than two Academy Awards.

Russell Albion Meyer was born March 21, 1922, in San Leandro, California, and was soon the product of a broken home. His receipt of a camera—a UniveX Cine 8—at the age of fifteen provided him with an escape route from his miserable family life.

This escape route became his life's work.

Already a film buff with several amateur films to his credit and an eye toward a career in moviemaking, Meyer enlisted at age eighteen in the U.S. Army Signal Corps. He parleyed his experience into learning motion-picture photography in an army school at MGM, then qualifying for an assignment as a military newsreel cameraman.

In 1944, his training finished, Meyer was assigned to the 166th Signal Photographic Company and sent to Europe to cover the advances of Bradley's First Army and Patton's Third Army as they battled their way across France and into Germany during the brutal winter.

(During one memorable weekend when he was nursing a leg mangled in a jeep accident, Meyer claims he met Ernest Hemingway, who treated him to the favors of a certain French lass so that, given the heavy combat he was facing, he would not risk dying a virgin.)

One night he accompanied General George Patton to shoot the newsreel footage of a secret mission. Patton had assembled a strike force to dart across the enemy lines and capture Hitler, who was believed to be visiting the front. The report turned out to be false, and Hitler was not captured. Patton issued dire warnings to anyone who spoke of the raid, and Meyer was denied the greatest newsreel scoop in history.

Nevertheless, Meyer covered the Battle of the Bulge, the advance through the Ardennes Forest and on to Germany, constantly coming under fire while capturing the combat on film.

Two of his most memorable sequences include a tank battering its way through an occupied building, and a young German soldier, scared out of his wits, surrendering to an Allied soldier who kicks him in the seat of his pants. His footage of the destruction of the French town Maizières-les-Metz after nearly thirty days of continuous battle is also quite impressive, and infinitely more action-packed than anything presented in *Saving Private Ryan*.

As a result, some of Meyer's filmwork was so good it wound up being included in the 1945 short-subject *Eisenhower: True Glory* and the 1970 big-budget military blockbuster *Patton*, both of which went on to win Academy Awards.

Exempting his own filmmaking work, Meyer also contributed indirectly to another major Hollywood film that garnered several Academy Award nominations. On one of his assignments he stopped to film a group of U.S. soldiers (mostly African American) who were undergoing commando training in a military stockade. A superior officer ordered the film to be confiscated. Later some military personnel explained to Meyer that these men had all been sentenced to death following court-martials and, in lieu of their sentences, were being prepped for a mission behind the lines in France.

Meyer shared this story with E. M. Nathanson, who turned it into his bestselling novel *The Dirty Dozen*. The book provided the basis for the film of the same name, which did a huge international box office and also secured an Oscar for Sound Effects Editing, and nominations in other technical categories as well as a Supporting Actor nomination for John Cassavetes.

In the movie, the officers and a single member of the dozen survived.

"In the real story," Meyer said, "they disappeared and were never heard of again."

Meyer never fell out of touch with his fellow combat cameramen, and he often held reunions of his old company, where there would always be plenty of free passes to the next big Russ Meyer film.

Vince Lombardi did not go out as a winner

"**W**inning is a habit."

"There is no substitute for work; it is the price of success."

"Football is a game of inches, and inches make a champion."

And as memorialized at the beginning of the Oliver Stone movie *Any Given Sunday:*

"But I firmly believe that any man's finest hour, his greatest fulfillment of all he holds dear, is the moment when he has worked his heart out in a good cause and lies exhausted on the field of battle—victorious."

These are just some of the words of wisdom uttered by the greatest football coach of all time, Vince Lombardi, a man synonymous with the desire and dedication to win, and, of course, with that emblematic NFL team from Wisconsin, the Green Bay Packers.

Consider the following list of accomplishments:

- He never had a losing season as head coach.

- His Packers won five championships over the span of nine years.

- He was the only coach to win three consecutive NFL championship games (1965, 1966, and 1967), and his Packers won the first two Super Bowls.

- He tallied a career coaching record of 105–35–6
  (regular and postseason combined), including a
  98–30–4 record in Green Bay.

It is no surprise that the Super Bowl trophy itself is named the Lombardi Trophy.

Born in New York City, Lombardi graduated from St. Francis Preparatory High School in Brooklyn, New York, and, in 1937, played football at Fordham University. He and his teammates ran up a string of twenty-five straight victories, and in many of the games their opponents went scoreless. (The Fordham front line, of which Lombardi was a member, became known as the Seven Blocks of Granite.)

Lombardi started his career as an assistant coach for Fordham University and later coached at West Point under Earl Blaik. He then became offensive coordinator for the New York Giants in the mid-1950s. Lombardi coached offense, while future coach of the Cowboys during their America's team/dynasty years Tom Landry coached the defense. Jim Lee Howell was head coach, but the two future Hall of Fame coaches created a fanatical loyalty within each unit that drove the New York Giants to repeated NFL championships.

Lombardi didn't get his first head coaching job until he was forty-five years old.

February 2, 1959, Lombardi arrived in Green Bay and told the committee, "I want it understood that I am in complete command here." Technically he wasn't, not yet, but within two days of his arrival, Tom Olejniczak, who was in charge of the Packer front office, gave Lombardi not only the head coaching job, but the vacant general manager position as well.

Lombardi's first season with the Packers was a success, turning that 1–10–1 team of 1958 into a 7–5 team in 1959 and picking up unanimous coach-of-the-year honors in the process.

And the rest of his career as a Packer speaks for itself and commands great respect that can never be taken away from the man.

But the awful truth is that he did not end his career as a Packer.

Having made his mark in Green Bay, he retired to the front office after the legendary Ice Bowl of 1967, retaining his position as general manager until that fateful day in 1969 when he dictated the following letter to his secretary (as cited by David Maraniss in *When Pride Still Mattered: A Life of Vince Lombardi*):

"It is with sincere regret and after many hours of deliberations that I am requesting a release from my contract with the Green Bay Packers. . . .

"My decision was based upon a number of factors. One was the equity position with the Washington Redskins and I do not believe I need to go into the advantages of capital gain position under today's tax laws. . . .

"There has never been a question of remuneration. After making a decision a year ago not to coach, I think you can all well understand the impossibility of my returning to the field in Green Bay. It would be totally unfair to coaches and players alike."

The Washington Redskins hadn't had a winning season in thirteen years, and undoubtedly represented a welcome challenge for the win-driven coach . . . but to paraphrase the sage, "when they say there has never been a question of remuneration, you know that it is about the remuneration," and the equity position in another team was obviously something that was unavailable at Green Bay.

So "Saint Vince" left the snowy field of Lambeau in search of greener pastures.

And in return for the effort, for their first Lombardi season, Washington still didn't crack a win ratio of more than 50 percent, which the Packers had managed during his first year in Green Bay, then continued to better each and every year after that.

It was also to be Lombardi's last year coaching; he was soon stricken with cancer and died the following year.

In exchange for an equity share, the man who was a god in Green Bay went out a loser.

And another awful truth about Lombardi: the most famous quote attributed to him wasn't even his own. Legendary actor

John Wayne actually uttered the phrase "Winning isn't everything, it's the only thing!" in a 1953 film called *Trouble Along the Way*, but it was a sentiment Vince was more than willing to embrace with his heart, mind, and soul, though maybe not his bank account.

There is no room for second place. There is only one place in my game and that is first place. I have finished second twice in my time at Green Bay, and I never want to finish second again. So let's get out there and show them what the Ladybugs are made of. Remember, winners never quit and quitters never win!

Packers shares are only ceremonial

One of the signs of true aristocracy in American society is prestigious and ostentatious ownership, whether of a television station, a record label, a line of fashion merchandise, or, among the fiscally crème de la crème, a movie studio or an organized sports franchise.

Indeed, many overgrown lads with way too much money indulge their adolescent dreams of sports glory through either the sole acquisition of a team (like George Steinbrenner with the New York Yankees or Mark Cuban with the Dallas Mavericks) or a partial share in a team (like multibook bestselling author Tom Clancy with the Baltimore Orioles or George W. Bush with the Texas Rangers).

Some actually turn a profit with their organizations.

Others don't.

And that's okay, because no one buys a team as an investment with the expectation that there is real money to be made.

It's a high-end vanity piece.

A rich man's toy.

Just another bauble to set apart the superrich from the rest of the masses.

That is, unless you live in Green Bay, Wisconsin, where their multichampionship NFL franchise is wholly owned by the town and their fans with strict limitations in place to prevent any single individual or manufactured coalition of individuals from assuming control of the team.

Indeed, the team has averted four financial collapses: 1921, 1922, 1934, and 1950, each time gaining monetary support from the community, leading to an aura of stability and mutual loyalty that is as true today as it was back in the 1920s. Presently, 111,921 people (representing 4,749,925 shares) can lay claim to a franchise ownership interest, and in an era of money-hungry franchise movement, where teams often relocate in search of better tax breaks, a new stadium, or better broadcast rights and luxury boxes, only ten other pro-sports teams—none in football—have held the same moniker in the same location longer (nine baseball, one hockey).

The Green Bay Packers corporation is that successful anomaly whose ownership model is strictly discouraged from future (or present, excluding the Packers) use by any other NFL franchise, expansion teams and relocated old teams inclusive.

The last stock sale for the team occurred on November 13, 1997, with the approval of the NFL, when the then existing 1,940 shareholders overwhelmingly voted to amend the articles of the corporation. The vote authorized raising funds for capital improvements, and shareholders received a 1,000 to 1 split on their original shares, allowing the Packers to sell up to 1 million newly issued shares.

The initial response to the stock offering was staggering. In the first eleven days, roughly one-third—or $7.8 million—of the total amount transacted was sold, an eccentric sale of such celerity that it is surpassed only by the speed with which Jerry Garcia sold out a limited Broadway run of classical guitar shows.

All die-hard Packers fans wanted to own a piece of their team, and this group's orders came from all across the country and well beyond to U.S. holdings in the Pacific, and included numerous celebrities in the mix such as Fox News personality Greta Van Susteren.

And indeed, all stockholders are created equal, and they stay that way no matter who they are.

They can look upon their stock certificate with pride as they root for their team . . . and that's about it.

You don't get to hire or fire the coach like the spoiled big boys do.

You don't get to redesign the team uniforms.

You don't even get a break on tickets (despite the fact that the 1923 stock sale included the compulsory stipulation that each stock purchaser also had to buy no fewer than six season tickets to help with the team's very necessary fund-raising).

Moreover, shares of stock cannot be resold, except back to the team for a fraction of the original price, and transfer of shares to heirs and relatives as part of an estate or as gifts is permissible only under certain circumstances.

There is an annual meeting of stockholders held in Green Bay each July to oversee the election of the board of directors . . . and that's about it; the board leaves the running of the team to the trained professionals (a model from which other owners might profit, given its commonsense approach to success).

Thus, the awful truth is that being a Green Bay Packers shareholder is largely just a ceremonial position, with no hopes for profit, power, or aggrandizement.

And that's just fine with Packers fans.

By the way, according to the official Green Bay Packers' website: "Based on the original 'Articles of Incorporation for the [then] Green Bay Football Corporation' put into place in 1923, if the Packers franchise was sold, after the payment of all expenses, any remaining monies would go to the Sullivan-Wallen Post of the American Legion in order to build 'a proper soldier's memorial.'" This stipulation was enacted to ensure that the club remained in Green Bay and that there could never be any financial enhancement for the shareholder. The beneficiary was changed from the Sullivan-Wallen Post to the Green Bay Packers Foundation on the basis of a shareholder vote at the November 1997 meeting.

And thus, for as long as there is a Green Bay, Wisconsin, there will be a team named the Green Bay Packers.

The Awful Truth

is
That These
Cartoon Rock-and-Roll Divas'
Singing Voices

Honey Bear *of The Sugar Bears*

Melody *of Josie and The Pussycats*

&

Ann Margrock *on The Flintstones*

Were Actually Voiced by

Kim Carnes

Cheryl Ladd *(under the name Cheri Moore)*

&

Ann-Margret

Chuck Berry's only #1 hit was "My Ding-a-Ling"

"**I**f you tried to give rock and roll another name, you might call it 'Chuck Berry,' " said John Lennon, and he was undoubtedly right.

Whether it was his masterful guitar work, his innovative "licks," his dynamic "duck-walking" stage performances . . . or just the plain fact that he epitomized rock and roll, Chuck Berry was and is the icon for everything that came after him in rock-and-roll music. Such is his prominence in the field that superstars like Bruce Springsteen, Keith Richards, Steve Miller, and Eric Clapton have all been willing to play behind him in concert as part of his backup band.

Born Charles Edward Anderson Berry on October 18, 1926, in St. Louis, Missouri, Berry was one of the first people inducted into the Rock and Roll Hall of Fame at its opening in 1986, and, despite a criminal record that included a violation of the Mann Act (for transporting a minor across state lines for sexual purposes), for which he served time in prison, and a 1979 charge of income tax evasion, he was also awarded a Kennedy Center Honor by the president of the United States in 2000.

Chuck Berry's recording of "Maybellene" (1955) fully synthesized the rock-and-roll music form, as a combination of blues and country music with teenage-centric lyrics—usually about girls and cars—alongside distinctive electric-guitar solos and an energetic boogying stage persona. His other classic hits (many of which have been covered by other great performers) include "Johnny B. Goode," "Rock and Roll Music," "Sweet Little Sixteen," "Roll Over Beethoven," "School Days," and "Too Much Monkey Business."

Yet the awful truth is that this giant of rock and roll had only one hit song that climbed to the very top of both the Billboard Hot 100 and the Cashbox Hot 100, and that was a novelty song that was recorded without his advance knowledge.

The song was the double-entendre-filled "My Ding-a-Ling." According to his autobiography:

On February 3, 1972, I was performing at the Lanchester Ballroom in Coventry, England, where another tricky tactic of the music industry's way of doing things without my knowledge was under way. At the close of my show, the song "My Ding-a-Ling" was recorded during my performance before thirty-five thousand students who eagerly, but also unaware, were joining in on the recording. I can't deny that it turned out okay but it would have been better for the band and myself to know if and when the recording was being made.

It is strange when I realize the magnitude that came from the song. I had been singing it for four years prior where audiences were appropriate and suddenly after recording it, it came to be number one on the record charts. What's more strange, at least to me, is that I had not registered a hit in seven years. In fact, after having two surges of popularity, I never expected to reach the top of the charts again.

The fact that the song was owned and published by Isalee Music Company, which was owned by Berry himself, allowed him to control the copyright and its licensing in a way that afforded him more leeway and profits than any of his previous hits.

Thus, even though it was a novelty song of questionable subject matter with perhaps the easiest guitar work of any of his hits, it became his only truly #1 hit . . . and perhaps his personally most profitable song to boot.

The fact that it was recorded without any extra effort or preparation beyond that which a life of performing on the road in front of rowdy audiences provides can only sweeten the rewards of "My Ding-a-Ling."

'Twas sex that saved the *Star Trek* franchise (and *Star Trek* and *Baywatch* have more in common than you might think)

Star Trek (pitched by its creator Gene Roddenberry as *Wagon Train* in outer space) originated as an NBC television series in 1966, but after two years of lackluster ratings, the show was threatened with cancellation, only to receive a one-year reprieve due to an aggressive save-the-show campaign by its loyal fans.

Though the show left the airwaves, its loyal following refused to consign it to some moldy grave, eventually making it one of TV's most successfully spun-off franchises in both major motion pictures and television syndication.

To date there have been five live-action *Star Trek* series and one animated series, altogether comprising (as of May 2005) a total of 726 individual aired episodes (not including the original pilot, which was unaired) and thirty seasons' worth of television, as well as ten exceptionally successful feature fims.

Baywatch began as a story concept from a former lifeguard who envisioned a television show based on his experiences. In 1989, *Baywatch: Panic at Malibu Pier* premiered on NBC as the highest-rated TV movie of the week. Excited, the network green-lighted a *Baywatch* series starring David Hasselhoff in an effort to catch that beach-bound wave of excitement into which the TV movie had tapped.

Many things had changed at NBC in the twenty years since the cancellation of *Star Trek*.

For one thing, shows were given a much shorter period in

which to prove themselves in the ratings, and, as a result, *Baywatch* was canceled after its first season's lackluster performance.

However, resurrection from the dead also occurred a lot faster, too, when the show's star revived it for the first-run syndication market in 1991, investing his own money and functioning as executive producer. (Hasselhoff truly believed that the show would find its audience and that success through syndication was more than possible, given the success of the new *Star Trek* TV shows, all of which were thriving without the support of the big three national networks: ABC, NBC, and CBS.)

The show continued to run through 1999, when it was replaced by a successor series called *Baywatch Hawaii*, which ran for two years, and a spin-off series with numerous crossover characters called *Baywatch Nights*. There was also a special-event TV movie called *Baywatch: Hawaiian Wedding*, and, in 2004, DreamWorks announced they had bought the rights to create a new theatrical *Baywatch* movie.

Though the die-hard fan groups of each of these two successful franchises have probably only a very small overlap in their membership, the legacy of the two shows have a lot more in common than one might think, and indeed, the powers that be that kept each franchise thriving may have looked to each other for helpful tips and lessons.

First, the blatant similarities:

Both shows were born on NBC, only to have the network abandon them due to ratings.

Both suffered from the perception of being down-market television based on subject matter considered to be the province of low-budget exploitation films (e.g., science fiction and beach movies), and as a result were no better than guilty pleasures for a chosen few.

Both thrived in the multiple-showing medium of syndicated TV.

Both fostered crossovers and spin-offs.

Both succeeded on an international basis as well as a domestic basis and, in some cases, generated more revenues overseas than in the United States.

Both fostered massive licensing deals that made the producers rich.

Second, the subtler similarities.

Both series made stars of its major players who were seemingly unable to parlay that success into other mediums. This is not to say that some of the performers did not find success elsewhere, just that it did not come easily. David Hasselhoff is still more popular in Europe as a solo performer than he is domestically. Pamela Anderson's first foray at stardom, *Barb Wire* (a T&A mercenary postapocalyptic version of *Casablanca*) was less than successful on a commercial basis both at the box office and as a video rental, not to mention the oblivion that awaited the after-*Baywatch* lives of Nicole Eggert, Donna D'Errico, Yasmine Bleeth, and numerous other bikini-clad beauties. Likewise, none of the *Star Trek* regulars met with immediate success in other venues (exempting those like Patrick Stewart, Brent Spiner, Rene Auberjonois, and Avery Brooks, who merely returned to their status as theatrical stage stalwarts of extremely ubiquitous abilities). Indeed, Leonard Nimoy and Jonathan Frakes both found more success behind the camera post-*Trek* than they had in front of it, and Canada's own William Shatner has endured close to twenty years of self-deprecating humor before reemerging as an in-demand, award-winning TV star.

The success of both series was usually overlooked at the Emmy Awards, and even die-hard fans sometimes feigned a certain amount of embarrassment that wound up manifesting itself on other TV shows, whether it was Cybill Shepherd doing a *Star Trek: The Next Generation* (*STNG*) cameo on her show, or just Joey and Chandler on *Friends* indulging in *Baywatch* must-see TV.

The lessons *Baywatch* learned from *Star Trek* were equally simple.

Hasselhoff expanded the franchise through a spin-off not dissimilar in theme (from adventure on the beach to mystery in the back alleys), with *Baywatch Nights* mirroring the spin-off of *Deep Space Nine* (*DS9*) from *STNG*, and then through a change of locale with *Baywatch Hawaii* in the vein of *Star Trek*'s *Voyager* spin-off—all very smart moves to expand the opportunities and keep the series from repeating what had been done in a previous incarnation.

And what did *Star Trek* learn from *Baywatch*?

A very simple lesson indeed.

When *Star Trek: Voyager* was beginning to prematurely wane in the ratings, never having achieved the same level of devoted following that the other *Trek* series had enjoyed, it was time for drastic action. A new character of complex nature was introduced, a humanoid whose alien-mechanized upbringing tapped into the logical yet naïve persona that was so popular in the previous characters of Spock and Data from the other series.

She was called Seven of Nine, a human-Borg construct, played by Jeri Ryan, who went from having the outward appearance of the illegitimate spawn of a transformer and a GI Joe to a Spandex-clad superbabe. Affectionatetly nicknamed "the booby borg" because of her noticeable natural endowments, her super-sexy appearance was coupled with a dominatrix-like attitude.

They had obviously learned that sex sells, and it did.

Star Trek: Voyager ratings turned right around, allowing the series to continue for a healthy run, comparable to the other shows in the franchise.

Jimi Hendrix was a former U.S. Army airborne paratrooper

The bandanna-bound headmaster of the guitar who brought the house down at Woodstock with his electrifying rendition of "The Star-Spangled Banner" and was embraced as a darling of the antiwar movement because of his revolutionary renditions of such songs as "All Along the Watchtower" and "Hey, Joe" actually seemed to lean a bit further to the right than anybody expected.

Jimi Hendrix was born Johnny Allen Hendrix, in Seattle, Washington, to Al Hendrix, a transplanted Canadian, and Lucille Jeter Hendrix, a mulatto of Irish Cherokee descent, in 1942. His father, after returning from World War II, changed his son's name to James Marshall Hendrix out of respect for the legendary military commander. (His parents divorced in 1951.)

Though his father was credited with exposing him to music at an early age, Jimi's abilities were more akin to those of a prodigy, and as soon as the young guitar player was old enough, he joined various area bands to refine his musical craft. He continued performing with the bands until a few altercations with the law (such as the occasional stolen car) led him to choose an enlistment in the military rather than a stint as a felon.

As a result, he enlisted in the army, joining the 101st Airborne Division (stationed at Fort Campbell, Kentucky) as a trainee paratrooper. There he underwent all the rigors that went along with airborne training, from jumping out of planes to learning marksmanship, and he proved himself to be far from an exemplary soldier.

To say that he was less than motivated would be an understatement.

What he really wanted to do was refine his musical craft, and, after a short term of service (enough to satisfy the legal authorities who had encouraged him to sign up), he was discharged and moved to Nashville, where he became a part of the burgeoning blues music scene, the evolution of which would later be known as soul music. From Nashville he made his way to New York, a recording contract, and meetings with such other revolutionaries of rock and roll as Frank Zappa; later he went to London, where he encountered the likes of Eric Clapton and Jeff Beck.

Guitarmanship doesn't let politics get in the way, not even during the Vietnam War, and though his Woodstock rendition of the national anthem was looked upon as a turning point in the American counterculture revolution, Hendrix's conscious contribution was probably solely of a musical nature, and probably devoid of any intentional social commentary.

Hendrix had been discharged from the U.S. Army three years before the Vietnam War saw large numbers of U.S. soldiers being sent to Southeast Asia. No matter what the grounds of his dismissal (medical or otherwise) were, antiwar feelings were not his primary motivation, if they existed at all, since there is no record of such feelings on his part at that time in his life. Strictly speaking, military service was just getting in the way of his guitar playing.

Though a proclaimed pacifist, it would probably be erroneous to label Hendrix antiwar. Close friends and acquaintances claimed that he held a seemingly prowar stance on Vietnam. Eric Burdon of the rock group The Animals (whose hits such as "We've Got to Get Out of This Place" eventually took on a decidedly antiwar cast) recalled that when Hendrix arrived in England, he spoke earnestly about the need for the United States to subdue Chinese Communism before it overtook the world. His personal values seemed to have stayed closer to those of his Washington State parentage, rather than those of the San Francisco "hippie" scene that lionized him as a god of the guitar.

Hendrix died on September 18, 1970, with the war still raging in Southeast Asia. His music was embraced by the peacenik flower children of the antiwar movement, and the American servicemen on Vietnam tours of duty, many of whom had shared a stint at Fort Campbell at some time during their paratrooper training.

Hendrix was a part of both worlds, and neither side could claim him as exclusively its own.

He was every bit as much of a man of the Right as he was of the Left . . . and perhaps the real truth of the matter is that he didn't really care.

Another interesting bit of right-wing irony occurred during his stay in New York in the mid-1960s.

In 1966, while he had his own band—Jimmy James and the Blue Flames—Hendrix got to know rock guitarist Jeff "Skunk" Baxter. Baxter eventually embraced the conservative/right-wing agenda and earned himself a reputation as an expert in matters of security, national and otherwise, with consultation gigs for such diverse groups as the Pentagon and the UN . . . and Jimi most likely would have had no problem with that at all.

Mario Puzo had no mob ties prior to publishing *The Godfather*

When one looks back at the twentieth century, there are two phenomenally successful pieces of bestselling fiction that have become firmly ensconced in the pantheon of that era's pop culture.

For the first half of the century, the book was Margaret Mitchell's *Gone with the Wind*, the epic historical saga of an overly romanticized Confederate South that never really existed.

For the second half of the century, the book was Mario Puzo's immigrant success story of honor, organized crime, and corruption, *The Godfather*, which not only became a metaphor for the dishonesty and lack of integrity of the American establishment, but also became the first popular look into organized crime that did not resemble a bubblegum portrayal one found in an episode of the TV series *The Untouchables*.

Gangsters like "Scarface Al" Capone and Frank Nitti were replaced by the Corleones and Luca Brasi; Eliot Ness, the law-and-order good guy, was replaced by . . . well . . . no one. This was a story without cop heroes.

Multitudes read between the lines of Puzo's potboiler, hoping for some clue to where the fiction stopped and facts supplied filler.

Was Johnny Fontaine really Frank Sinatra, and did it take a horse's head in someone's bed to get him the part in *From Here to Eternity*?

Which New York–based olive oil importer was really a mob front?

Readers had already been treated to bits of mob history like Albert Anastasia getting hit in a barber shop in such memoirs as *The Valachi Papers*—surely Puzo was relating real events with the names changed to protect the guilty.

Wasn't Michael Corleone really Bill Bonanno, the new generation of mafiosi who would eventually inherit his position as one of the original five families?

And to what family was Puzo "connected"?

Surely he had to be connected . . . how else could he have been able to describe the secret world of organized crime in all of its familial glory?

Some publishing insiders even circulated the rumor that Puzo had been paid an exorbitant amount of money beyond the advance by certain ranking members of La Cosa Nostra who wanted to be assured that the *Family* would be cast in only the most flattering and sympathetic of lights.

Borrowing from Puzo's own mob lexicon—it was alleged that they had made him an offer that he couldn't refuse.

So the question remains how this less-than-prosperous literary author gained entrée into the highest ranks of organized crime.

The answer is simple.

He didn't, or rather, as he stated after the book was published:

> I'm ashamed to admit that I wrote *The Godfather* entirely from research. I never met a real honest-to-god gangster. I knew the gambling world pretty good, but that's all. After the book became "famous," I was introduced to a few gentlemen related to the material. They were flattering. They refused to believe that I had never been in the rackets. They refused to believe that I had never had the confidence of a Don.
>
> —from *The Godfather Papers and Other Confessions*

Puzo also admitted that he wrote the book for one reason only—the money—and indeed looked down on this book as sub-par to his two previous novels. He even occasionally regretted that he didn't devote enough care and craft to the work (the publisher allegedly went to press with his first draft), and had he known how many people would wind up reading it, he might have done a better book.

"I starved before the success of *The Godfather*. If I was in the Mafia, I would have made enough money so I wouldn't have had to write it," said Puzo.

This admission on his part did not stop the rumors that he was connected, and indeed the celebrity of the book and its commercial success as a film vastly widened his circle of questionable acquaintances (including the friends of Frank Sinatra—Sinatra, who was personally offended by the slanderous depiction of himself in the fictional character of Johnny Fontaine, an allegation of inspiration that Puzo firmly denied).

Never before had there been such an insightful view into the day-to-day lives of members of the Mafia, far surpassing such previous nonfiction peeks as *The Valachi Papers*.

Everything seemed so real and so immediate.

Later on, Puzo did make two confessions.

First, he acknowledged that his focus on the Corleone family life and its emphasis on honor and integrity may have been a bit romantic, and that perhaps he may not have given sufficient time to the vice, buffoonery, and thuggery that went hand in hand with day-to-day mob existence.

Second, he acknowledged that there *was* a real person who had provided the inspiration for the infamous man of respect and family, Don Vito Corleone, the Godfather.

Was it Salvatore Maranzano, the first Boss of Bosses in the United States?

Perhaps Joseph Profaci, or maybe Joseph "Joe Bananas" Bonanno?

None of the above.

It was Puzo's mother.

As he admitted in an interview: "My mother was a wonderful, handsome woman, but a fairly ruthless person."

Charles Manson did not personally take part in the Helter-Skelter slaughter

When he was released from prison in 1967 at the age of thirty-three, Charles Manson had spent most of his adult life in prison, mostly for offenses such as car theft, forgery, credit card fraud, and pandering . . . and the worst was yet to come.

Within four years he was convicted of first-degree murder for the infamous Tate/LaBianca slayings, also known as the Helter Skelter murders, and on March 29, 1971, he was sentenced to death.

The murders had achieved a level of notoriety in the international press. Among the victims were Sharon Tate—the starlet wife of internationally renowned film director Roman Polanski—who was eight and a half months pregnant, celebrity hairstylist Jay Sebring, and wealthy supermarket executive Leno LaBianca and his wife, Rosemary . . . but more than by the celebrity status of the victims, the public was transfixed by the level of inhuman savagery of the murders themselves.

Manson's visage stared back from the page ones of newspapers all over the world—the convicted murderer grinning in satanic defiance.

But the awful truth of the matter is that Charles Manson did not actually commit any of the killings himself.

The murders were committed by his followers.

They were called the Family (dubbed such by Vincent Bugliosi, the prosecutor and author of the definitive book on the case,

Helter Skelter), a commune bound together by fanatical loyalty to Manson and a negation of all conventional moral precepts.

Soon after his 1967 release from prison, Manson moved to Los Angeles, at first basing himself and the Family in the seaside community of Pacific Palisades, then moving to the western San Fernando Valley to the unused Spahn Ranch, which had been formerly used to make Westerns.

Once there, he began preaching to his ever-growing number of loyal disciples based on inspiration he discerned from the lyrics of the songs on the Beatles' so-called *White Album*. His generic message to the converts usually focused on an impending race war and nuclear holocaust with signs and portents dating back to biblical prophecy. The bottom line was always that his word was law; he was their god.

(During this time he also tried to establish himself as a rock/folk singer through connections with such music insiders as Dennis Wilson of the Beach Boys, but to no real avail.)

Somewhere along the way the charismatic messiah persona merged with the psychopathic criminal in such a way that the two were indistinguishable to his followers. Minor crimes like drug dealing, trespassing, and so forth were soon replaced with extortion, robbery, and murder (there is ample evidence to suggest that the Tate/LaBianca murders were not the first slaughters engineered by the Family). But though evidence of Charlie's psychopathic rages and hate speech were evident to all who met him, there was little evidence to connect him to any of the actual criminal acts (presumably in accordance with his own careful planning, given his criminal record and the likelihood that he would probably be sent back to prison for even the most minor of legal infractions).

His "Family" for the most part followed his orders to the letter, even though most of the acts they perpetrated were anathema to their, largely, upper-middle-class backgrounds. Through Charlie they rejected the establishment and all of the conventions associated with it.

Thus, on the night of August 9, 1969, when Charles Manson directed some members of the Family to commit homicide for homicide's sake, they assented immediatetly and followed his orders.

At or around midnight, they entered the grounds of the Beverly Hills home of the Polanskis. Polanski, who was out of the country, had asked friends to stay with the very pregnant Tate. Before entering the house, the Family members shot dead Steven Parent, an eighteen-year-old friend of the Polanskis, and then proceeded to brutalize and slaughter the posh home's inhabitants, even tracking down and killing one couple who tried to get away.

The next night Charlie led them to a home in the Los Feliz section of Los Angeles, where he instructed them on a more efficient way to conduct their slaughter, but then left before the actual killing took place.

Initially the two cases were investigated independently, but eventually the police zeroed in on the Manson Family, and arrested them all, including Charlie.

During the trial Manson and his followers seemed more concerned with attracting attention and shocking onlookers than in actually mounting a defense. At one point Charlie showed up at the courthouse with an X carved into his forehead with a knife. This action was copied by his followers the next day. Charlie modified the pattern several times, with his disciples following suit each time. Eventually he settled on a swastika pattern (which is now a permanent scar). These sort of mind games only strengthened the prosecution's case that Charlie had complete and utter control over his disciples and was therefore directly responsible for their actions even when he wasn't physically taking part in them.

In the end, eight members of the Family were convicted of nine murders in the first degree (though the suggestion was clear that these nine, while enough to convict with a death sentence, were probably only the tip of the homicide iceberg of killings perpetrated by Charlie and his disciples).

Thus, even though Manson himself was not proved to be present at the Tate/LaBianca killings, he was convicted of first-degree murder on January 25, 1971, for ordering and directing them, and on March 29 was sentenced to death. (The death sentence was later automatically commuted to life in prison due to the California Supreme Court's *People vs. Anderson* decision, which resulted in the invalidation of all death sentences imposed in California prior to 1972.)

Manson has never shown remorse and, as a result, will likely never be let out of prison. Though his hands might be physically free of bloodstains on the surface, there is no denying his part in this savage conspiracy, nor is there any doubt that without him this senseless slaughter would never have happened.

Elvis Presley was profoundly antidrugs

On August 16, 1977, Elvis Presley, the King of rock and roll, was found dead in his bathroom at Graceland Mansion.

He was only forty-two.

There was much speculation about how a man so young—though obviously overweight—could just suddenly die, and the immediate cause of death (as was reported) suggested that he had had a heart attack during the strain of a bowel movement, possibly caused by some previously undiagnosed cardiovascular disorder that might have been exacerbated by his weight problem.

A further investigation and autopsy concluded otherwise.

The King was dead from an overdose.

The coroner reported the presence of "significant amounts" of "codeine, methaqualone, ethinamate, and miscellaneous barbiturates" as well as "traces of morphine, Valium, Demerol, Meperidine, Placidyl, and chlorpheniramine" in his system. (The coroner also noted that Elvis's last meal had consisted of four scoops of ice cream and six chocolate chip cookies.)

Very soon thereafter, numerous articles, books, and exposés began to reveal the life of excess that Presley had been living for over a decade.

The irregular schedule of Presley's life on the road had led to his suffering chronic bouts of insomnia, which necessitated the use of sleeping pills to get rest after a long night of partying. He followed those by a few hits of Dexedrine the following afternoon in order to wipe away the narcotic grogginess, allowing him to perform again that night. Add to this a regimen of pain pills for the wear and tear on his body from both his weight gain and the martial arts he did for show preparation and personal amusement, as well as mood stabilizers to combat depression and a host of other pharmaceuticals. It would be easy to conclude that Elvis Presley was the equivalent of a walking drugstore.

But the awful truth of the matter is that Elvis never considered himself to be a drug addict, nor did he consider himself even to have a slight drug problem.

On the contrary, the King always considered himself to be profoundly antinarcotic, and he often spoke disparagingly of those who did indulge in recreational drug use. Moreover, the King wanted to take an active role in the emerging war on drugs Washington was talking about, so he reached out to President Nixon in hopes that he could lend a hand.

A meeting was arranged, and on December 21, 1970, Elvis Presley paid a visit to Richard M. Nixon at the White House in Washington, D.C. At the meeting Presley suggested that the president officially appoint him a "federal agent-at-large" in the Bureau of Narcotics and Dangerous Drugs.

Following the meeting, White House staffers conceived an idea wherein Elvis could compose a song with the theme "Get High on Life" and then record the track at the Public Health Services hospital in Lexington, Kentucky (home to a federal narcotics rehabilitation and research facility), but for some reason the project never went through.

In no way, shape, or form was Elvis Aaron Presley being a hypocrite.

Presley was not taking drugs illegally.

Every pill he took was authorized with a prescription.

(Although his personal physician, Dr. George C. Nichopoulos, was exonerated in Presley's death, in July 1995 he had his license suspended after the Tennessee Board of Medical Examiners found that he had improperly dispensed potentially addictive drugs to a variety of his patients, a practice that undoubtedly contributed to Presley's problems.)

As noted by Jerry Hopkins in one of his several Presley

biographies, "Elvis regarded his many prescriptions as medicine. He had real problems—pain, insomnia, a tendency toward obesity—and he was taking real medicine to take care of those problems. And that was it."

The pills were prescribed by a doctor, and therefore they had to be all right, or so the King thought. The doctor knew what he was doing, so why worry?

This is not to say that Elvis took his pills only for medical reasons. Even the King himself was never that self-deluded.

At the same time, if a doctor gives you a pill to fill you with pep or to make you feel happy, delirious, or just plain good, where is the harm? This is why you need to have a good doctor always available, and by making such pills available, those good doctors are merely doing their jobs, earning their fees.

Elvis trusted others to look out for his own best interests.

They didn't.

And as a result he was killed by a drug problem he never knew he had.

Billie Jean King vs. Bobby Riggs: A true battle of the sexes?

It was billed as the Battle of the Sexes.

On September 20, 1973, two Wimbledon triple-crown winners squared off at the Houston Astrodome for a tennis match that was supposed to be the ultimate battle of the sexes, an event that would change the course of both sports history and male-female relations, striking a blow for that which was called at the time "women's liberation."

There was much left to prove then.

Women were not receiving equal pay for equal work.

Women were not afforded the same athletic scholarship opportunities as men.

And, quite frankly, no one paid as much attention to women's sports as they did to men's sports. True, most people could name a famous female athlete (usually Babe Didrikson), and plenty of people tuned in for the gymnastic events at the Olympics, falling in love with that year's Cathy Rigby or Olga Korbut, but compared with the viewership for the MLB, NBA, and the NFL, the women's audience was clearly dwarfed, perhaps even by golf, the most visually boring televised sport ever.

And as a result, women athletes received much less exposure and earned substantially less than their male counterparts.

It was indeed a sore spot for women professional sports players that not only were they paid so much less than men, but they were not even afforded the courtesy of competitive negotiation. This was why the Women's Tennis Association, a union of women players, was formed in hopes of improving their bargaining power . . . and one of its founders was Billie Jean King.

Among her accomplishments:

- She won twenty titles at Wimbledon.

- She became the first woman to make $100,000 in tennis.

- She was the Associated Press's Woman Athlete of the Year in 1967 and 1973.

- She was *Sports Illustrated*'s Sportswoman of the Year in 1972.

- She was *Time* magazine's Woman of the Year in 1976.

She was at the height of her game and had the highest profile of any female athlete.

So when the second-seed female tennis champ (Margaret Court) was soundly beaten by a male tennis hustler in a $10,000 winner-take-all match dubbed the Mother's Day Massacre, it fell to King to prove once and for all on nationwide television that women could do more than compete with men; women could beat men fair and square on the battlefield of sports.

King's opponent, the same guy who challenged her and trounced Court, shared the status of being the only other Wimbledon triple-crown winner—the only difference being that he won his in 1939, and she won hers in 1973, thirty-four years later.

Indeed, the comparable profile male players of the Billie Jean King era were fellows with names like John Newcombe, Stan Smith, Ilie Nastase, and Arthur Ashe. True, none of them dominated the field as consistently as King did women's tennis, but a competitive field at the top never hurt any sport.

But none of those names were considered or even issued challenges.

The male challenger in the Battle of the Sexes was fifty-five-year-old Bobby Riggs (ranked #1 in 1939), whose early expertise at tennis had given way to a more lucrative career as a hustler on the court and off.

To say that he was not at the top of his form would be kind.

To say that he was interchangeable with Ashe, Nastase, or any of King's male contemporaries would be absurd.

Who he was didn't really matter.

He was a male chauvinist tennis pro of respectable legacy with an aptitude for showmanship.

He was the perfect straw man to prove the point.

Beat him and declare that equality of the sexes had been established on the tennis court. That was all that really mattered.

In addition to the age factor, Riggs also managed to weaken his own position on the court, using the run up to the match as an opportunity for moneymaking promotions and public relations. While King was practicing, he was granting interviews. While she was resting, he was schmoozing. While she was concentrating on her game, he was concentrating on her.

As a hustler, Riggs knew that the advantage lies with the one who manages to get into the opponent's head. Most of his previous wins had involved tactically getting his opponent off position and then scoring points with his drop shot (considered by many to have been the best move of its type of all time) from both the forehand and the backhand. Adding to this was his ability to psych out his opponent in advance through intimidation, aggravation, and distraction. Among his favorite "tricks" were playing in a dress around obstacles set up on his side of the court, or playing with self-imposed limitations such as using backhand return shots only.

His 6–2, 6–1 victory over Margaret Court landed him on the cover of both *Sports Illustrated* and *Time* magazine, even though the fault for her loss lay squarely in her own camp because she had inadequately prepared for the match. She had underestimated her opponent and had allowed herself to be distracted by his antics.

She was playing out of anger—she was not playing to win.

Billie Jean King did not make any of these mistakes. She isolated herself from the pregame sideshow and played strictly to win . . . which she did in three straight sets: 6–4, 6–3, 6–3.

But the awful truth is that this was not the *real* battle of the sexes, where the victorious side could declare dominion over the loser. To say that Billie Jean beating Bobby meant that women were better at tennis than men was the equivalent of saying that Great Britain's victory in the Falklands reestablished the United Kingdom as a world military power.

Bobby Riggs was not representative of the top male tennis player. A few decades earlier, maybe, but in 1973, never . . . and he knew it, which is why he was no longer a competitive player on the tennis circuit, playing only for exhibitions and show events. Billie Jean might have been the best women's tennis had to offer, but Bobby was just a guy who happened to show up to play her.

This is not to belittle the Battle of the Sexes match or its place in history as a monumental event in the evolution of women's rights.

What it did do was perhaps more important than resolving the male vs. female issue.

First, it proved that there was a huge box office for sports involving women.

Second, it reaffirmed that women would not necessarily crack under pressure on camera.

Third, it opened up the dialogue between men and women on the subject of sports in a way that never existed before.

As to the competitors themselves, Bobby Riggs reestablished himself in the limelight as a personality and a hustler worthy of late-night talk-show notoriety. Even though he lost, he won.

For Billie Jean King, the victory helped to cement the advances that were already taking place. In her words, "I was nervous that maybe they would go back on Title IX if I lost that match. I know how things can change very quickly . . . and I knew the hearts and minds of people weren't matching Title IX.

"Bobby Riggs was a true friend for the last twenty-five years," she said upon his death. "It [the match] helped a lot of people realize that everyone can have skills, whether you are a man or a woman."

Sometimes even well-hyped media events do some good, even if the outcome is not as black-and-white as the initial billing might suggest.

All in the Family's Ancestry

There is no greater symbol of the 1970s' American television sitcom than Norman Lear's *All in the Family*. The show broke all sorts of cultural barriers in its humorous yet pointed look at the tensions of the blue-collar American family in the evolving world of the post-1960s social revolution.

The big-mouthed, small-minded bigot Archie Bunker; his wife, Edith ("Dingbat"); daughter, Gloria; and son-in-law, Mike ("Meathead") struck a chord that earned the show the kind of critical success and mass appeal as more than evidenced by its consistent landing in the top ten of Nielsen ratings.

It even produced a whole far-flung family of spin-offs, many of which succeeded at a comparable level.

The *All in the Family* legacy of spin-off shows include *Maude, Archie Bunker's Place* (basically *All in the Family: The Sequel*), *The Jeffersons, Gloria* (failed spin-off of the character of Gloria), *704 Hauser* (failed spin-off featuring an African American family living at the Bunkers' old address), *Good Times* (spin-off of *Maude*), and *Checking In* (failed spin-off of *The Jeffersons* character Florence).

The show even earned an exhibit at the Smithsonian Institution's Museum of American History in recognition of its enormous resonance with its viewing audience.

The argument can be made that there was no more American television show at its time than *All in the Family*.

But the awful truth of the matter is that the true origins of the show reach far across the pond, and this distinctively American show was actually the revisioning of a British sitcom.

Lear's inspiration was the British show *Till Death Us Do Part,* which basically broke the bigotry barrier with its depiction of a narrow-minded proletariat-type bigot coping with modern society, with his family life as the show's focus.

Lear innovated the concept.

Politics changed from Liberal and Conservative to Democrat and Republican, football (really soccer) fandom was replaced by baseball, immigrants from the East moving into the neighborhood became African Americans and Hispanics, the pub became the bar, and so on, but the Archie archetype, for which Lear was so roundly praised, had its roots in its British predecessor.

This Anglo ancestry was easily overlooked by many of the narrow-minded Archie Bunker types who helped to make the show a success. Many fans disparaged British shows, the so-called PBS fare of the upper crust. They liked their shows distinctly American . . . just like Archie.

Norman Lear meanwhile reworked his successful formula for *All in the Family* by Americanizing yet another successful British series. *Sanford and Son* enjoyed a successful five-and-a-half-year run, during which it consistently ranked in the top ten, one year coming in at number two, right below *All in the Family.* The producers' attempts at spin-offs (*Grady,* and *The Sanford Arms*) and a sequel series (*Sanford*), however, failed miserably. The show was based on the British series *Steptoe and Son* (dealing with a similarly low-class and crass father-and-son antiques/junk dealership), though Lear innovated that original concept by going with African American actors as the principals. This might have been the key to its success because its network NBC touted the show as the African American answer to CBS's *All in the Family.*

Three's Company, the T&A sitcom that launched the superstar careers of John Ritter and Suzanne Somers, had a similar British legacy. The show was a remake of the British sitcom *Man About the House* and revolved around two women and a man sharing an apartment. Though *Three's Company* was a huge success for seven seasons, unlike its Anglo counterpart, an attempt at a sequel series (*Three's a Crowd*, based on *Robin's Nest*) and a spin-off series (*The Ropers*, based on *George and Mildred*) failed miserably.

Though all of these shows are distinctly American, one cannot overlook their ancestral roots across the pond . . . perhaps not unlike our nation's own roots.

Sacheen Littlefeather: Acting "stand-in" for Brando

There are usually three events of Academy Award history that the tabloids trot out each year to typify the unexpected and spontaneous surprises that have been known to occur. In reverse order of outrageousness, they are:

- Jack Palance's one-armed push-up demonstration during his acceptance of the Best Supporting Actor award

- David Niven's comment, "The only laugh that man will ever get in his life is by stripping . . . and showing his shortcomings," after a streaker whizzed by him

- Marlon Brando's nonacceptance of his award for Best Actor in *The Godfather*

On March 27, 1973, the nominees for Best Actor that year were Michael Caine and Laurence Olivier for *Sleuth,* Peter O'Toole for *The Ruling Class,* Paul Winfield for *Sounder,* and Marlon Brando for his role as Don Corleone in *The Godfather.*

The winner was announced by Roger Moore and Liv Ullman. Brando won.

A young woman in beaded doeskin took the stage at the Dorothy Chandler Pavilion, in Los Angeles, California, to read a prepared statement from Brando in the place of his acceptance of the award. Prior to the announcement, the woman had been told that the star's statement was way too long, and, as a result, she was forced to extemporize on the spot:

> Marlon Brando . . . has asked me to tell you, in a very long speech which I cannot share with you presently—because of time—but I will be glad to share with the press afterward, that he must . . . very regretfully cannot accept this very generous award. And the reason for this being . . . are the treatment of American Indians today by the film industry . . . excuse me . . . and on television in movie re-runs, and also the recent happenings at Wounded Knee. I beg at this time that I have not intruded upon this evening and that we will, in the future . . . our hearts and our understanding will meet with love and generosity. Thank you on the behalf of Marlon Brando.

The immediate reaction was shock, then amusement (including such memorable quips as Clint Eastwood wondering whether he should present the award for Best Picture "on behalf of all the cowboys shot in John Ford Westerns over the years"), and then bitter indignation at the perceived insult to Hollywood's yearly night of honor and respect.

But the awful truth is that this young Indian maiden who had been taken advantage of by eccentric method actor Brando and enlisted to deliver his message was actually an actress named Maria Cruz (who had previously been named Miss American Vampire in 1970, and parlayed her fifteen minutes of scandal and fame into a few roles in such movies as *The Trial of Billy Jack* and *Winterhawk* and an appearance in *Playboy* magazine). She was not, however, as described by John Wayne, "some little girl dressed up in an Indian outfit." No matter what her name was, she was truly of Native American lineage. Far from being the "faux Apache" that media outlets later claimed, she was actually part Apache, part Yaqui, part Pueblo, and part Caucasian, and she used her notoriety to further Native American causes.

Moreover, Brando's perceived slight of the awards was a last-minute thing, possibly caused by his own insecurities and the potential for embarrassment if he showed up and didn't win. Littlefeather (a tribal name that actually had been bestowed on her) was an on-again, off-again platonic guest in the Brando household, and she happened to be there when the star decided against going himself, and designated her and his secretary Alice Marchak as his surrogates.

It is also noteworthy that the speech Brando had intended Littlefeather to read specifically said, "I do not feel that I can as a citizen of the United States accept an award *tonight*," thus tempering his remarks so that it wouldn't come across as a condemnation of the awards, which was implied by George C. Scott's refusal of his Oscar for *Patton*. Add to this the protests over the poor conditions at Indian reservations and the injustices the government had perpetrated over the years at Wounded Knee, which Brando had taken to heart, as well as the severe depression he felt over the recent and unexpected death of his close friend and former roommate, Wally Cox, and one might have to conclude that, rather than the huge publicity-grabbing insult depicted by the press, the event was more likely just an exercise in poor judgment during a time of personal stress. Brando himself conceded years later, "If I had to do it all over again, I'd probably handle it differently."

George Lucas's lifetime achievement

George Lucas was the recipient of the 2004 American Film Institute Life Achievement Award.

But George Lucas has directed only six major motion pictures:

- *THX 1138*

- *American Graffiti*

- *Star Wars*

- *Star Wars: Episode I—The Phantom Menace*

- *Star Wars: Episode II—Attack of the Clones*

- *Star Wars: Episode III—Revenge of the Sith*

That's it.

Of course the list would be considerably longer if we included all post–initial release revisions as new films (the so-called "Special Editions"), but that just wouldn't be fair.

Six films, a record on par with such great American filmmakers as Penny Marshall and Robert Redford . . . though one could argue that their best works are not more than twenty-five years old.

And at best reasonable critics have him batting .500.

What about as a producer?

True, he produced the *Indiana Jones* franchise and numerous successful knockoffs of *Star Wars*, including the animated *Clone Wars, Droids,* and *Ewoks* series, and the memorable *The Star Wars Holiday Special* . . . but he also produced such intended franchise hopefuls as *Howard the Duck* and *Willow*.

And let's not forget that marvel of marvels Captain Eo, done in 3D for the Disney theme parks and starring Michael Jackson.

What did he do as a writer?

Radioland Murders.

What did he do in other areas?

Robert Redford started the Sundance Institute. Steven Spielberg started the Shoah Foundation. And Lucas? He set up computer games.

Beyond that?

He produced special effects for other filmmakers.

Any other accomplishments?

Nada.

So how does this one-trick pony stack up against the true masters of filmmaking?

Master of the epic form on film? He can't hold a candle to Akira Kurosawa, David Lean, or Cecil B. DeMille.

Special effects? Ray Harryhausen got there first.

Bloated budgets with every dollar evident on the screen? Dino De Laurentiis.

Even the American filmmaker with whom he is most often compared, Steven Spielberg, has shown a greater depth of palette in his work, ranging from the crowd-pleasers like *Jaws* and *E.T.* to the more thoughtful dramas of *Schindler's List* and *Munich*.

So why do we revere George Lucas as a great filmmaker? Probably for the same reason some people think of Donald Trump as a mover and shaker.

Celebrity and flash make an impression and win out over substance every time.

And the question remains: Does Lucas have another *Star Wars* or *American Graffiti* in him (and I'm not talking about yet another sequel or some such *Star Wars "Really" Special Edition*)?

Only time will tell, and twenty-five years is an awfully long time between new and original projects.

And now that the second (or is it first) *Star Wars* trilogy is over . . . was that worth the wait?

Well, it took three movies to get us to the plot point where the first movie started and a quality level not quite equal to the third movie in the series (*Return of the Jedi*).

In the Victorian age, one of the public athletic attractions was a little race called a "wobble"—a marathon-like race held on an indoor wooden track, in which grown men would run/walk in a circle till they dropped or won the race after days of "wobbling" in one place.

Now that Lucas's "wobble" is over, maybe he can trot back to the wide open space and take advantage of a different landscape, a bit of fresh air, and perhaps some new inspiration.

But even if he does, it might not make it worth sitting through revised versions of *Willow* and *The Phantom Menace*.

I prefer to think of it as twenty-two years of character development for Jar Jar Binks.

Oliver Stone's horror debut

In the book *My First Movie: Twenty Celebrated Directors Talk About Their First Film,* by Stephen Lowenstein, Oliver Stone discusses in great detail his masterpiece *Salvador.* Though Stone had already won an Academy Award prior to this film for his *Midnight Express* screenplay, he had yet to enter the ranks of directors worthy of note and attention.

But the awful truth is that *Salvador* was not his first film.

True, he was not the director of *Midnight Express,* and most of his early noteworthy efforts on the screen were as a screenwriter, but, even so, *Salvador* was not his debut.

It was not even his second film.

His second film was titled *The Hand* (based on the novel *The Lizard's Tail,* by Marc Brandel), a surreal variation on *The Beast with Five Fingers* featuring Michael Caine as a graphic artist who believes that his dismembered and missing hand is seeking vengeance. It was a major studio release from Warner Bros. and should not have been inadvertently forgotten by Stone, since he even had a cameo in the film in the role of "the bum."

But, though *The Hand* was his first major studio directorial debut in 1981, it was not the first film he helmed and received directorial credit.

That occurred in 1974, four years before he received the Academy Award for Best Adapted Screenplay for *Midnight Express,* seven years before *The Hand,* and more than a decade before *Salvador.*

That film, Oliver Stone's directorial debut, was a very low-budget Canadian film titled *Seizure*.

Essentially, *Seizure* is a classic variation on the theme of a writer losing control of his imagination when his invented dream-world overlaps into his real world, shot as a horror film and done with a very post-1960s "what is real/what is fantasy" approach to sex and violence.

The film itself is noteworthy to film buffs on the basis of its cast alone. Among the players were:

- Jonathan Fridd—the legendary Barnabas Collins of *Dark Shadows* fame

- Troy Donahue—blond Adonis of such films as *A Summer Place, Parrish,* and *The Godfather: Part II*

- Martine Beswick—former Bond girl and Hammer/AIP horror babe

- Mary Woronov—member of the Warhol factory group and indie-cult star of *Eating Raoul, Rock 'n' Roll High School,* and *Death Race 2000*

- Christina Pickles—TV actress who gained prominence on *St. Elsewhere* and then went on to play Ross and Monica Geller's mother on *Friends*

- Herve Villechaize—playing Spider the demonic dwarf in this, his feature film debut; the diminutive thespian would go on to fame as Knick-Knack in *The Man with the Golden Gun* and as Tattoo on *Fantasy Island*

Moreover, there is really nothing to be ashamed of regarding the film's execution. Though it doesn't rank with comparable works of psychological horror such as George Romero's *Jack's Wife* (the first film from the director of *The Night of the Living Dead*) or Dario Argento's *Suspiria,* it is nonetheless an interesting low-budget horror film that indeed precedes several themes that auteurs such as Stephen King and Peter Straub would more fully execute.

The fact that it was shot on a shoestring budget, with minimal retakes, is to be expected in a first film . . . and not a sufficient reason to have this work ignored by its director as his truly credited "first" major motion picture.

The Awful Truth

is
That These Famous
Romance Authors

Jennifer Wilde (*author of* Love's
Tender Fury),

Marilyn Ross (*author of* Dark
Shadows *and* Love Is Forever),

&

Felicia Andrews (*author of*
Riverrun *and* Riverwitch)

Were Actually
Men

Tom Huff

William Edward Daniel Ross

&

Charles Grant

Gene Simmons of KISS fame was a teenage geek

When you think of Gene Simmons, what's the first thing to come to mind?

(Discounting the temporary sidetracking if you are over sixty-five and by mistake heard "Jean" Simmons, the virginal babe in such classic films as *Guys and Dolls,* Olivier's *Hamlet, Spartacus,* and *Elmer Gantry.*)

Perhaps KISS's fire-belching demon-spawn rock-and-roller front man, the one with the humongous tongue who could "rock and roll all night, party every day," or maybe you remember his 2001 acknowledgment that he had had more than forty-six hundred sexual liaisons over the course of his career (from his *New York Times* bestselling autobiography *Kiss and Make-Up*) and his long-standing open relationship with B-movie vixen Shannon Tweed, whom he met at the Playboy mansion.

Maybe you just remember the tongue that seemed to go on for feet rather than inches, and the assuredness with which he spoke when an interviewer would ask how long it was (a question to which he would usually reply, "Well, with you sitting over there and me sitting here, we could still become quite *friendly.*"

Perhaps you remember the archetypal evil villains he played in *Runaway,* bedeviling Tom Selleck and Cynthia Rhodes with robotically controlled bullets, or in the big-screen retooling of the TV series *Wanted Dead or Alive* as international Arab terrorist Al-Malik al-Rahim, who was dispatched with a live grenade in his mouth.

No matter how you look at it, Simmons is the quintessential embodiment of dark arts, metal, and cool.

It's hard to believe that he started life as a geek, but it's true.

Born August 25, 1949, in Haifa, Israel, Chaim Witz (the man who would become Gene Simmons) immigrated with his mother to America in the late 1950s and settled in the outer boroughs of New York City, where his name was soon changed to Gene Klein.

According to David Leaf and Ken Sharp in *KISS Behind the Mask: The Official Authorized Biography*: "Gene's days in this new and foreign land were basically divided into two parts. Every day for ten hours he attended a yeshiva . . . , in every other free moment Gene's attention was focused on his two new loves—television and monsters."

(Not exactly an auspicious beginning for the chick magnet he would become, though the affinity for monsters did seem to have an impact on his later career.)

Moreover, as Gene entered adolescence and became "more American," his tastes matured, too, as did his appetites, leading him to aggressively pursue the sensual pleasures of . . . fanzines?

In Gene's words (from *Sex Money Kiss*):

At age fourteen, I was completely immersed in science fiction and fantasy. I read voraciously: *Famous Monsters of Filmland* and *Castle of Frankenstein* magazines, *Analog* and *Amazing Stories Monthly,* comic books and books. I discovered an underground press of fans who published their own fan magazines known as fanzines. I started writing and drawing for these fanzines and would eventually go on to publish, write and edit my own fanzines.

Fanzines and fan-oriented letter writing were an inaugural stage for many soon-to-be celebrities, such as award-winning writers like Harlan Ellison and Roger Ebert, as well as such household names as Stephen King and Leonard Maltin . . . but somehow Gene Simmons doesn't seem to fit this mold.

Based on his image and stage persona, one can more easily visualize him as the bully who might steal and stomp on a young

Roger Ebert's glasses or purposely leave the junior high dance with the young Stephen King's date on his arm.

Make fun of the geeks and nerds? Sure.

But *be* one of them? Never.

Yet he was.

The man with the magnificent tongue edited no fewer than five different fanzines over the course of his adolescent career, and he entered into numerous cross-country correspondences with others of similar interest and ilk, using the moniker "Gene from Brooklyn." He even had his own rexograph (later traded in for the newer-model mimeograph) so that he could print his zines in his own basement.

Moreover, by his late teens, this soon-to-be rock star weighed close to 220 pounds.

In summation, the facts are that Gene Simmons:

• was a yeshiva student

• lived with his mother

• was an overweight teenager

• was a comic-book-buying, monster-loving fanboy

• was a fanzine fanatic

Had there been *Star Trek* and *Star Wars* conventions at that time, he probably would have been in attendance.

Had Dungeons and Dragons been invented yet, he would have played it.

He was a geek through and through.

Let this be a lesson to all adolescent boys with a tendency toward geekiness.

You, too, can go far—maybe even become an oversexed rock star—if you try hard enough, and, of course, if you are gifted with a phenomenally long tongue.

The "Not Ready for Prime Time Players" misnomer

When *Saturday Night Live* debuted in 1975, it christened its repertory company of performers who were contracted to appear and perform regularly each week as the "Not Ready for Prime Time Players," a moniker that seemed to have been inspired as a cross between the "Fresh Faces of . . ." from the days of Hollywood reviews and the in-house moniker for *Mad* magazine's staff talent (clearly labeled in the staff box as "The Usual Gang of Idiots").

Despite the self-deprecating label, many of the original cast members went on to become household names, such as John Belushi and Gilda Radner, and even as new members came and went, the moniker remained the "Not Ready for Prime Time Players."

Ironically, the label became increasingly inaccurate as the talent proved itself to be not just ready for prime time . . . but in some cases *better* than prime time.

In fact, the awful truth of the matter is that this group has included numerous Academy Award nominees.

The first member of the cast to earn this accolade was Dan Aykroyd, one of the six original members of the repertory group, whose memorable characters ranged from Elwood Blues (of the Blues Brothers) to Irwin Mainway, the shady pitchman of such products as the Big Box of Broken Glass—Every Child's Favorite Toy, to spot-on impersonations of Rod Serling, Jimmy Carter, and Bob Dole. In 1990 he garnered the first Academy Award nomination for a Not Ready for Prime Time Player alumnus for his supporting role in Bruce Beresford's *Driving Miss Daisy.*

Bill Murray, who joined the group in its second year, has since one-upped Aykroyd with a Best Actor nomination for his part in Sofia Coppola's 2005 *Lost in Translation* . . . though it must be noted that his was not the first such nomination for a member of the company. This accolade belongs to a cast member who was on *SNL* as part of the company for only a single season, 1985 to 1986, and is not immediately associated with *Saturday Night Live*—his Hollywood exploits both onscreen and off have attracted more attention than his short-lived stint on the show. Indeed, Robert Downey, Jr. received a nomination for Best Actor in 1993 for the eponymous title role in *Chaplin,* and he won the British equivalent for that year and that part.

The so-called *SNL* class of 1985 also included another distinguished thespian whose involvement as a Not Ready for Prime Time Player has been all but forgotten. Joan Cusack has in fact been nominated for not one but two Academy Awards in the Supporting Actress category, the first as best friend/coconspirator in 1989's *Working Girl,* and the second as the semi-oblivious bride to be in 1998's *In and Out.*

This class also included another Academy Award nominee of distinction whose achievement renders truly ironic the "Not Ready" moniker, even more so because he had already earned an Academy Award nomination almost twelve years prior to his joining the company. Though Randy Quaid even outside of *SNL* is primarily remembered for his buffoonish parts in such movies as *Independence Day* and the *National Lampoon's Vacation* series, he did earn an Academy Award nomination in the Supporting Actor category for his part as a court-martialed seaman on his way to prison in 1974 in *The Last Detail,* which starred Jack Nicholson.

There is yet another Academy Award nominee among the *SNL* alumni . . . but not in the acting category.

Michael McKean first came to public attention as part of the over-the-top doofy twosome of Lenny and Squiggy in Garry Marshall's successful spin-off from *Happy Days, Laverne and*

Shirley. His later work with Christopher Guest on Rob Reiner's rock-parody documentary *This Is Spinal Tap* made him a natural for the *SNL* cast. His stint on the show lasted from 1993 to 1995 while he continued development on numerous other projects, including future collaborations with Guest on *Spinal Tap Reunion* and the dog show parody *Best in Show*.

McKean received his Academy Award nomination as part of collaboration on a film he did with Guest . . . though the nominated collaboration was not with Guest but with McKean's real-life wife, actress Annette O'Toole. The film was the folk-music reunion parody *A Mighty Wind,* and the nomination was in the Best Song category for the McKeans' songwriting joint effort "A Kiss at the End of the Rainbow."

Numerous other *SNL* alumni have garnered other accolades for their achievements off the show, including non-*SNL* Emmys (the *SNL* Emmys are too numerous to mention) for Laurie Metcalf (a partial-*SNL*-season cast member in 1980 to 1981) for her part as Jackie in *Roseanne* and Chris Rock (1990 to 1993) for his HBO show, literary awards for Al Franken, and even Tony and Obie nominations for Julia Sweeney and Colin Quinn, to name but a few.

The alums' seven Academy Award nominations is a noteworthy achievement more than befitting Prime Time status, a point readily recognized by fellow rep member Billy Crystal (*SNL* member from 1984 to 1985), who has hosted the Oscar-night festivities no fewer than eight times, and has never received a single nomination for his own work on the silver screen, a point he himself bemoaned in 1993 when David Paymer was nominated in the Supporting Actor category for the film *Mr. Saturday Night*, which starred and was directed by Crystal. This was the second time in two years that Billy found himself in a similar situation; Jack Palance had won in the same category the year before in another Crystal film, *City Slickers,* and, to add insult to injury, he upstaged Crystal that night by garnering the greatest volume of belly laughs with his one-armed push-ups onstage as part of his acceptance speech.

All in all, definitely worthy of Prime Time.

Patrick O'Brian, the Irish seafaring author who wasn't

E very decade brings a new overnight success that was decades in the making. Usually it is an author who has been writing for years, gradually accumulating a dedicated following, who suddenly "clicks" with a certain book that then propels him to overnight bestsellerdom.

In the 1970s it was Louis L'Amour.

In the 1980s it was Elmore Leonard.

And in the 1990s it was Patrick O'Brian, whose overnight success is even more surprising, given that it was for books in a series that two publishers had tried previously to market successfully in the United States to no avail.

The series was centered on an unusual twosome, a naval officer and a ship's doctor during the Napoleonic Wars.

The first volume appeared in 1969, after O'Brian, already well past fifty years of age (with six out-of-print novels and several volumes of short stories already behind him and forgotten by the reading public) accepted an offer from Lippincott to write a naval adventure set during the Napoleonic Wars. The first book had the unlikely title of *Master and Commander* and enjoyed a very modest success, so the author decided to continue the series, even after it was dropped by its U.S. publisher after the fifth book. The British audience had grown sufficiently to support the series continuation.

Jack Aubrey, the naval captain, is Horatio Hornblower in need of analysis, sanguine, openhearted, merry, a perfect fool ashore, and a daring and dauntless commander at sea. Stephen Maturin, half Irish, half Catalan, is brooding, sardonic, subtle, and brilliant; a "scientific philosopher" by choice, he is much more than ship doctor, a post that Aubrey convinces him to accept.

And as the books progress we gradually learn more about their lives and loves, and the secrets each man possesses.

It was only in the 1990s, after a dedicated editor at Norton (who was quoted as saying that one of the nice things about Norton Publishing was that they sometimes gave their editors enough rope to hang themselves if they really wanted . . . as was his case with O'Brian's work) convinced his higher-ups to relaunch the series in the United States by setting up a schedule that allowed the gradual release of the backlist of the series, along with the new books (starting with the twelfth) as they appeared in England.

Less than two years later the books began to crack the national bestseller list, and O'Brian was viewed as an overnight sensation.

Everyone wanted to know more about this nautical Irishman who eschewed interviews.

His author bio in a nutshell was as follows:

He was born in 1914 into an Irish Catholic family of some distinction. His early years were filled with the social niceties of French lessons, books, horses, travel, foxhunting, and a governess, but by the Great Depression his people had fallen on hard times.

His mother died when he was a child, and a lung illness, which troubled him into adulthood, sometimes kept him at home, where he was privately tutored. A voracious reader, he once found a chest full of unbound copies of *The Gentleman's Magazine,* an eighteenth-century publication edited for a time by Dr. Johnson, which he devoured.

At some point he went to sea, perhaps the sea air was the recommended cure for his illness, and he spent a good part of the next phase of his life as a sailor. A relative owned a two-ton sloop, and other friends had boats. But best of all, one family acquaintance owned a converted bark-rigged merchantman, which offered the opportunity to "hand, reef, and steer" in the old manner.

Somewhere along the way he mastered a peripatetic education, including the Sorbonne, and grounding in the natural sciences and the classics. O'Brian speaks French, moderate Irish, Catalan, Spanish, Italian, and Latin.

A stint driving ambulances during the blitz, intelligence work with the French resistance, and other suggested bits of excitement preceded his embrace of the writing profession, where he gained prominence as a translator.

He moved to France, married the Countess Tolstoy, and set about making himself a successful and published author who guarded his privacy.

And guard his privacy he continued to do, even after he hit the big time, first in England, and then in the United States . . . and there was a good reason for it.

Because the awful truth of the matter is that substantial portions of his author bio were total fiction.

Patrick O'Brian was born Richard Russ, a sickly, very non-Irish child born to a bankrupt, eccentric German doctor who was always coming up with failed contraptions—such as a cure for venereal disease that involved electrocuting the sufferer's bladder. His non-Irish mother died of TB when he was four, leading to an even meaner boyhood existence in Great Britain.

The seafaring stories came from a loquacious uncle, and the derring-do hero prototype probably from his brother, both providing fertile fodder for his imaginative mind.

He married an illiterate Welsh woman and fathered a child who was diagnosed with spina bifida.

World War II did provide him a chance to work for British intelligence in some bureaucratic position, and also the opportunity to meet Countess Tolstoy, with whom he had an affair that eventually led to his leaving his wife and dying child, filing for divorce, changing his name, and breaking with all aspects of his previous life. He married the countess and settled in France to raise a new family and embroider a new "Irish" past that was far better than the one he had experienced.

He did achieve success as an English translator of French, including such impressive works as some of the writings of Simone de Beauvoir, a definitive biography of Charles de Gaulle, and the international prison-break bestseller *Papillon*. In addition, he authored a well-received biography of Pablo Picasso.

It would appear that his new life agreed with him a lot more than his previous life.

It gave him room to grow as a writer, and the opportunity to take forty years to become a bestselling overnight success on both sides of the Atlantic.

Embroidering fiction is a necessary talent for a writer, but not all of them fabricate their lives as well.

The inauspicious beginnings of *Seinfeld*

In 2002, *TV Guide* released a list of the top fifty greatest shows of all time and ranked *Seinfeld* number one.

The show's finale was watched by an estimated 76 million viewers.

Its stars (Jerry Seinfeld, Jason Alexander, Julia Louis-Dreyfus, and Michael Richards) have become synonymous with the characters they portrayed (Jerry, George, Elaine, and Kramer) . . . and their combined residual income from the show could finance a small state's government.

The show itself holds the record for the highest television advertising rates, and Jerry Seinfeld holds both the record for the "most money refused," according to the *Guinness Book of World Records*, by refusing an offer to continue the show for $5 million per episode, and the record for highest ever annual earnings for a TV actor.

But the awful truth of the matter is that the now-immortal fantastically popular show about nothing was almost canceled, and this soon-to-be jewel of the NBC Thursday-night lineup was actually offered to Fox after its initial lackluster ratings were noticed.

Jerry Seinfeld's previous record on TV was undistinguished, if not mediocre at best. His stand-up routine had caught the eye of Rodney Dangerfield, who later included him in his HBO special, which led to an opportunity on a successful TV sitcom . . . but what was originally supposed to be an ongoing character part on

Benson (where Seinfeld played a joke writer for Benson's employer, the governor) was abruptly curtailed. The character was not written out of the storyline in the middle of the 1979 season, just deleted from existence, the TV equivalent of being let go with extreme prejudice.

Thus, as a result, he returned to the ranks of numerous other stand-up comedians hoping to make it big.

After months back on the road Seinfeld made a splash following a highly successful appearance on Johnny Carson's *The Tonight Show*, and then similar gigs on *Late Night with David Letterman* and the *Merv Griffin Show*.

As a result, he had the opportunity to try the sitcom world once again, though this time he wouldn't really be expected to act since the character he was supposed to play was himself—and the purpose for the stand-up excerpts that bookended each show was that the show would be about how a comedian gathers material for his act.

The show was to be called *The Seinfeld Chronicles*.

It premiered on May 31, 1990, on NBC, and it was far from an immediate success. Indeed, prior to the airing of the pilot (on July 5, 1989) a pickup by NBC did not seem likely, and the show was actually offered to Fox, which declined. It was only thanks to Rick Ludwin, head of late night and special events for NBC, who diverted money from his budget, that the next four episodes were filmed, allowing the show its initial trial run on the schedule.

Jerry Seinfeld and cocreator Larry David realized that they had an uphill climb ahead of them, and that a sitcom about a stand-up comic was not exactly a lock on compelling television programming.

Show business was a tricky subject for TV.

For every *Make Room for Daddy* (which focused around the family life of a nightclub singer) and *The Partridge Family* (the family life of a rock group), there was always a *Hello, Larry* (the family life of a disc jockey) or *A Year at the Top* (a Faustian look at the pop-music scene) . . . and *Seinfeld* lacked the family foil from whence most of the humor originated.

Seinfeld had nothing except an ex-girlfriend and a nebbishy buddy who was the embodiment of failed mediocrity . . . and, later on, an eccentric neighbor across the hall.

As a result, Seinfeld and David shifted the focus away from the established norm of making everyday situations funny, substituting in its place the funniness of everyday "ordinary" situations . . . like waiting for a table in a Chinese restaurant, shot in real time.

The network executives wanted to know what was going to happen.

"Nothing," they replied.

And the executives were not pleased, but since they expected the show to be canceled anyway, they indulged the idiosyncratic creators.

What failed to resonate with the execs struck a chord with the viewing audience, and the so-called show about nothing blossomed in both a creative sense, with such classic episodes as "The Contest" and such memorable characters as Newman, Puddy, and, of course, the Soup Nazi, and in popular acclaim, securing dominance in its time slot week after week.

Stephen Ambrose and his war-hero dove

For most of the 1990s Stephen Ambrose was the number-one bestselling American historian.

In the post-Vietnam generation, the public turned away from the war movie as a genre, but his classic chronicles of the Allied Forces under Ike in World War II rekindled America's love affair with the everyday soldier-heroes of the Greatest Generation and paved the way for a cinematic renaissance of the heroics of World War II, which included such big-screen productions as *Saving Private Ryan* and *Pearl Harbor,* and such mammoth TV productions as *Band of Brothers.* Whether his books dealt with the officers under Ike, the citizen-soldiers, or the coordination of the D-day invasion, Ambrose's readers embraced the "war-hawk" within as they returned to those martial days of yesteryear.

The last major book of Ambrose's career as a military historian was titled *The Wild Blue: The Men and Boys Who Flew the B-24s Over Germany 1944–45.* It dealt with a different "band of brothers," the very young men who flew the B-24s over Germany in World War II facing the terrible odds in their flights against the dreaded Luftwaffe, and the Nazi antiaircraft guns (not to mention the unavoidable incidental risks of mechanical failure and exposure).

In the words of the flap copy:

Ambrose recounts their extraordinary brand of heroism, skill, daring, and comradeship with the same vivid detail and affection. Ambrose describes how the Army Air Forces recruited, trained, and then chose those few who would undertake the most demanding and dangerous jobs in the war. These are the boys—turned pilots, bombardiers, navigators, and gunners of the B-24s—who suffered over 50 percent casualties. With his remarkable gift for bringing alive the action and tension of combat, Ambrose carries us along in the crowded, uncomfortable, and dangerous B-24s as their crews fought to the death through thick black smoke and deadly flak to reach their targets and destroy the German war machine.

And as always in an Ambrose book, a certain character comes to the forefront, one whose individual heroic accomplishments in a time of war sets him apart from the rest of his band of brothers.

And the awful truth of the matter is that in *The Wild Blue* that master warrior turned out to be a young flyer named George McGovern . . . the same George McGovern who was the Democratic nominee for the presidency in 1972, running on an antiwar platform against incumbent-president Richard Nixon, still aggressively enmeshed in the Vietnam conflict. Three key elements of McGovern's platform were a unilateral withdrawal from the Vietnam War in exchange for the return of American prisoners of war, amnesty for draft evaders who had left the country, and an across-the-board 37 percent reduction in defense spending over three years. He also was one of the early supporters for the ratification of the ERA (Equal Rights Amendment) at a time when a good portion of the electorate considered it to be unmanly.

Not only was he defeated in the election, he was also derided as a dove, a peacenik, and a wuss—definitely not, therefore, the typical poster boy for the dedicated hawkish audience that had made so many other Stephen Ambrose books bestsellers.

What no one thought to mention at the time, however, was that he had also volunteered for the U.S. Army Air Forces during World War II and served as a B-24 Liberator bomber pilot in the Fifteenth Air Force, flying thirty-five missions over enemy territory from bases in North Africa and later Italy, often against heavy antiaircraft artillery.

He had also been awarded two Distinguished Flying Crosses for his service.

Ambrose doesn't flinch in the details and realism as he chronicles George McGovern's experiences as a pilot during the last months of World War II, when he flew his missions out of a base near Cerignola, Italy: during this time McGovern made three emergency landings, saw his copilot killed in action, and endured as the crews of other planes, his fellow band of brothers, often went down in flames right before his eyes.

Thirty-five was the maximum amount of missions a pilot was allowed to fly in that theater in a B-24, and most of the missions proved to have casualty rates in excess of 50 percent.

McGovern, soon to be the antiwar candidate, flew the maximum number of missions successfully and with distinction. He was undoubtedly an outstanding war pilot. By including McGovern's story in *The Wild Blue*, whether authorially advertent or not, this popular chronicler of martial matters proved that, though a leopard might not be able to change its spots, it was indeed possible for even the most successful of hawks to become a dove.

GOP as Big Government party

Not an election cycle goes by in which the Republican Party hasn't campaigned on such platitudes as "the GOP is the party of limited government and fiscal restraint," while the Democrats are "the Big Government party filled with tax-and-spend liberals."

This is the GOP mantra, and its alleged legacy since it emerged as the party of Abraham Lincoln in the mid-nineteenth century.

And since those early days, the moniker has been grossly inaccurate.

Indeed, the term "New Deal," usually disparaged by Republicans as Franklin Delano Roosevelt's "Big Government crusade," was actually first coined during the Lincoln years by a North Carolina newspaper editor to describe the federal deal Lincoln offered the border state to rejoin the Union during the last year of the war. The entire Lincoln-era presidency was filled with programs that initiated a rapid growth spurt in governmental powers, programs, and payroll logs, for example, the inauguration of the federal income tax and several new tariffs; innovations to the transportation and postal systems, including the railway mail service, "free" urban mail delivery, and expanded postal service— and the institution of the postal money order system; new governmental departments and bureaus, including the Office of Immigration, the Bureau of Printing and Engraving, the Department of Agriculture, and the National Academy of Sciences; as well as far-reaching governmental acts, including the Homestead

Act, the Morrill Land-Grant College Act, the Transcontinental Railroad Grants, the National Banking Acts, and the Contract Labor Act.

From a loose standpoint, all of the federal acts related to post–Civil War Reconstruction also can be viewed as an expansion of federal government and its powers.

Another GOP poster boy of Big Government was Theodore Roosevelt, who signed the Pure Food and Drug Act of 1906, doubled the number of national parks, strengthened the Interstate Commerce Commission, and encouraged labor reform and a graduated income tax.

Prohibition, great experiment that it was, and the only amendment to the Constitution that wound up being specifically repealed rather than amended, was also a Big Government innovation of the Republican Party.

True, all of this government expansion nurtured by the GOP took place prior to the reign of FDR. He adapted his own Big Government plans to meet the needs of the growing American society and nurture a progressive sense of egalitarianism to combat the perceived inequities of the alleged Gilded Age and the subsequent Great Depression that it ushered in. FDR further fostered federal powers out of necessity when his administration quickly turned the nation around into a focused war economy at the advent of World War II.

Perhaps one can argue that when the Republican Party castigates Big Government, it is overlooking those expansion acts that might have been a necessary part of historical development, or, in simpler terms, Abraham Lincoln, Theodore Roosevelt, and Herbert Hoover were merely responding to specific and timely concerns that bedeviled their tenures rather than fostering a philosophy of the type of indiscriminate government expansion undertaken by Franklin Delano Roosevelt and Lyndon B. Johnson.

Let's take a look at a more recent era of history—the age of the Republican resurgence to power that began with the Reagan revolution and continues today during the terms of Bush the Younger.

True, Ronald Reagan advocated the elimination of the Departments of Education and Energy, and offset increases in the Defense budget, with cuts to domestic programs to yield a pseudo break-even budget, but many of his efforts were hampered by a Congress that was largely controlled by the opposition party.

In the so-called Contract with America in 1994, the GOP committed to a restoration of fiscal responsibility to an out-of-control Congress that would now have to live under the same budget constraints as private businesses and families. In other words, you don't spend money you don't have or have already allocated elsewhere.

Such promises allowed them to seize control of Congress, but since the presidency was in the hands of the tax-and-spend Democrats, their fiscally responsible efforts could never produce fully realized Republican results.

This makes for a perfect "talking point" excuse at election time, if it weren't for the facts pointed out by Major Garrett in his book *The Fifteen Biggest Lies in Politics*:

> In their first three budgets [of the 1990s], Republicans increased federal spending by $183 billion, compared to a three-year increase of $155 billion racked up by a *Democratically controlled Congress*. That's right, Republicans in charge of the nation's purse strings have devoted more to domestic spending than Democrats did while working with Clinton. . . . In 1998 alone Republicans increased non-defense spending by $22.6 billion. That translates into a ten percent increase in non-defense spending over 1997.

Still one can always blame this on the give-and-take of divided government control.

The president got some of his priorities funded, Congress got some of its, and there was probably very little real overlap.

It was a give-and-take situation, and compromise was required on all sides.

This, of course, changed with the election of 2000, when both houses of Congress and the White House became firmly ensconced in Republican hands, thus allowing for a fully concerted implementation of a program of governmental downsizing and fiscal discipline in line with the precepts of the platforms the GOP had been campaigning on the last quarter of a century.

But this concerted implementation never took place.

In its place were such Big Government programs as the No Child Left Behind Act (roughly the antithesis of the abolition of the Department of Education, as proposed by Reagan), a new subsidy-filled Farm Bill (that nullified the intent of the 1996 GOP-sponsored Freedom to Farm Act), and a Medicare Prescription Drug Program (that was low-balled beyond belief in terms of its overall expense). There was also the creation of a new cabinet department—the Department of Homeland Security—which involved the federalization of numerous private jobs, the consolidation of several agencies, and an overall governmental bureaucratic expansion that is still evolving.

Yet again, the situational exigencies of the moment can be used as an excuse.

The attacks of 9/11, the resurgence of recession, and so on, have all played a role, and have necessitated several bold federal moves.

Surely the GOP would follow the Reagan model, offsetting these new expenses with budget reductions elsewhere.

Such is not the case.

Discretionary spending is way up.

So-called "pork projects" are attached to every bold move, sometimes as incentives for support, other times as payback, and sometimes for no good reason at all. (Need I mention the quarter of a million dollars that was allocated to a town in Missouri to discourage the alleged expansion of "goth" culture?) And business subsidies ("corporate welfare," in Democrat speak) are also on the rise.

There are even moves with the dominant GOP party to extend the government's involvement in people's everyday life in the name of security and/or public morals.

Thus, it would appear that Big Government is infinitely non-partisan, and that it is wrong to overspend a taxpayer's money only when the other party makes the decision how to spend it.

Big Government is here to stay.

It's never gone away, not since the age of Lincoln, no matter who controlled the White House or Congress.

To say otherwise would be tantamount to playing politics or, more simply put, telling a bald-faced lie.

In order to combat "Big Government" I have appointed
two commissions and a new cabinet post, and have established
the Department of Small Government Services…

Hip, off the hook . . . and based on a classic that's older than your parents

Hollywood is always aiming its product at the teen market. Teens are the ones with the time on their hands and the discretionary income to make a movie a blockbuster on opening weekend as well as assure a certain percentage of repeat business in the weeks thereafter.

The successful teen movie is usually one of the following:

- an action flick heavy on special effects or video game–like confrontation scenarios

- a lighthearted T&A comedy where young people frolic and find love and fun in typical teen settings

- a relevant-issue-focused film that manages to present a serious idea (like gang violence or racism) packaged as either a romance or action flick (as described in the previous scenarios)

It is this type of formulaic filmmaking that has made box-office blockbusters of such films as *The Warriors, O, She's All That,* and *Clueless,* all young-people-related films starring attractive young actors who will appeal to the hip, cool, and with-it audience.

But the awful truth of the matter is, to quote the Bard of Avon, there is nothing new under the sun, and indeed all of these films are based on works that are not just older than the parents of the target audience, but their grandparents as well.

For example, *The Warriors*, a classic action-packed film of gang violence from the late 1970s, which has recently experienced a resurgence in popularity due to an exceptionally successful video game tie-in, is actually based on the "Anabassis" of Xenophon, which was a contemporaneous historical account of an episode during the Persian War of the fourth century B.C., in which an army of Greek mercenaries must fight its way home from deep within enemy territory.

Likewise, *O*, a film dealing with prejudice, passion, and jealousy on an exclusive private-school basketball team—which was left on the shelf for two years following the Columbine shootings—is actually an update for teens of Shakespeare's classic *The Tragedy of Othello, the Moor of Venice*. The character O is not a mercenary but rather an inner-city basketball star who is enrolled in an elite private school on a sports scholarship; he becomes involved with the headmaster's daughter and is the object of a teammate's mortal jealousy.

Shakespeare is also the source for the memorable *10 Things I Hate About You*, which introduced Heath Ledger to teen heart-throb status. Here the tried-and-true story of *The Taming of the Shrew* (which had previously been modernized in the Broadway musical *Kiss Me, Kate* and the television series *Moonlighting*'s episode "Atomic Shakespeare") is relocated to a California 90210 high school with an appealing and pretty teen cast and a hot rock-and-roll sound track, without a name change for the shrewish heroine Kate.

Yet another reinterpretation of a previously reinterpreted work was the Freddie Prinze, Jr. and Rachael Leigh Cook starrer *She's All That*, the classic tale of a bet among friends that a BMOC (big man on campus) can transfom a nerdy weirdo into a prom-queen hottie with popularity potential. Its inspiration dates back further than the classic musical *My Fair Lady*, which immediately comes to mind, to the ancestor it shares with that Lerner and Loewe masterpiece, none other than George Bernard Shaw's 1912 play *Pygmalion*.

Clueless, with Alicia Silverstone, which launched both a successful spin-off television series and a second generation of valley girls, was a perfectly self-conscious comedy of courtship manners set among the kids of California's post-1960s beautiful people. As the rituals of dating and romance among young people change only in terms of the brand names worn and the gifts bestowed, it was highly appropriate that the source for the screenplay was the Regency era's queen of manners herself, Jane Austen, and her novel *Emma* (which was, coincidentally, remade as a period piece starring Gwyneth Paltrow within months of *Clueless*'s box-office success).

Needless to say, you can't go wrong stealing your inspiration from the classics, and not just in terms of teen films either.

Lest we forget the Coen Brothers' film *O Brother, Where Art Thou?*, which starred George Clooney.

Though the Coens derived its title and subject matter from a throwaway line in Preston Sturges's *Sullivan's Travels*, the actual plot of the film dates back quite a bit further to Homer's classic epic poem *The Odyssey*.

Joe Torre's less-than-enthusiastic New York reception

On May 8, 2005, Joe Torre reached nine hundred career wins as manager of the New York Yankees. This was just another milestone in a stellar baseball career whose final destination will undoubtedly be a place in the Baseball Hall of Fame in Cooperstown, New York.

As a player Torre had already made his mark.

In 1971, as a player with the St. Louis Cardinals, he led the National League in two triple-crown categories—runs batted in, or RBIs (137), and batting average (.363)—as well as in hits and total bases. He was named the National League's Most Valuable Player and an All Star. In total he received four more All-Star selections (1970 to 1973) while with the Cardinals. Following the 1974 season, he was traded to the Mets, where, on July 21, 1975, he set the National League record for most double plays grounded into in a single game: four.

However, it was only after he had retired as a player that his ascendancy to the ranks of baseball greats was assured. When he was manager, he led the Yankees to six American League pennants and four World Series titles, turning around a team whose high payroll had previously produced low-rent results.

Joe Torre was heralded as the man who saved George Steinbrenner's Yankees, and he emerged as a hero to millions of New York fans who longed for their team to return to its prior greatness, leading his team to the playoffs each year from 1996 to 2005.

But the awful truth of the matter was that Torre's initial reception in the Big Apple was far from enthusiastic.

Prior to his tenure at the Yankees, Torre had previously managed the Braves, the Cardinals, and the Mets, each time with less-than-spectacular results. There was even a gap between his managerial assignments during which he had to bide his time as a broadcast announcer in order to keep his profile noticeable in case any new managerial opportunites became available.

On November 2, 1995, he was chosen by Steinbrenner to helm the flailing-about New York Yankees in hopes of turning the tide (despite the fact that his entire experience in baseball as both a manager and a player had been confined to the National League, and the Yankees were part of the American League).

To say that Torre was not exactly a hot property was an understatement, and Steinbrenner was known for his demanding manner and willingness to change managers at whim.

Indeed, the position of Yankees manager was usually considered to be a short-term assignment, with a life expectancy not unlike that of a World War II kamikaze pilot, and conventional wisdom at the time was that Torre's tenure in New York might be shorter than the time it would take to travel crosstown.

The *New York Daily News* heralded his arrival with the now-famous tabloid headline CLUELESS JOE. The sports cognoscenti seemed to be equally divided between those who felt he had nothing to lose, given his lackluster managerial career, and those who felt that he was so "clueless" he might not even be aware of the viper pit he was diving into as a manager under Steinbrenner.

And Yankee fans were a far-from-forgiving lot, having suffered through the tantrums of Billy Martin, and the high priced–low performance stars that made up baseball's team with the highest payroll.

Immediate results were demanded.

And Torre complied, flabbergasting all who predicted his failure.

In 1995 he led the team to a Wild Card berth.

In 1996 Torre made his first-ever trip to the Fall Classic, leading the Yankees to their first World Series championship since

1978. After losing in the American League playoffs in 1997, the team raced back with three straight World Series titles in 1998, 1999, and 2000.

Torre nurtured the careers of rookies such as Derek Jeter, Bernie Williams, and Andy Pettite, and he helped turn around the careers of such past-their-prime former stars as Darryl Strawberry, David Justice, and David Cone . . . and along the way he returned the Bronx Bombers to the cocky excellence their fans demanded.

Joe Torre's Baseball Hall of Fame career as a player has been debated greatly—he is considered to be just slightly below the elite level of skill that warrants election. He is accomplished, worthy of respect . . . but does not necessarily have the superstar status that the Hall of Fame requires.

However, based on his accomplishments as the Yankees' manager, he is more than likely to be elected at the first available opportunity following his retirement.

Meanwhile the headline CLUELESS JOE rivals DEWEY BEATS TRUMAN in the annals of journalistic boo-boos.

J. R. R. Tolkien did not invent Middle-Earth

Every Christmas from 2001 to 2003, U.S. audiences saw the premiere of a critically acclaimed box-office smash that was, in reality, only one-third of an epic motion picture rather than a stand-alone or a self-contained episode à la the *Indiana Jones* series or the latest incarnation of *Batman, Spiderman*, or some other comic-book character.

These smash films were set in Middle-Earth.

The three movies were *The Lord of the Rings: The Fellowship of the Ring*, *The Lord of the Rings: The Two Towers*, and *The Lord of the Rings: The Return of The King*, and, all told, the films, as directed by Peter Jackson, garnered seventeen Academy Awards. The third made a sweep of eleven awards, tying it with two other films for the most single Oscars won in a given year. This three-part cinematic blockbuster, however, was the culmination of many years of work, all reaching back to the author of the most popular fantasy trilogy of all time, J. R. R. Tolkien.

John Ronald Reuel Tolkien (January 3, 1892–September 2, 1973) conceived of *The Lord of the Rings* as a single book published in three volumes. It is an epic story of hobbits (halflings with furry feet), elves, dwarfs, orcs, and other fanciful creatures taking part in a cataclysmic battle between good and evil. The story is filled with memorable characters such as Bilbo and Frodo Baggins; Gandalf the Grey; Gollum; Saruman; and Aragorn, the heir to the throne. All of them inhabit a magical world called Middle-Earth.

Though it has inspired numerous imitations (and quite

possibly the entire commercial genre of what we now know as epic high fantasy), none have ever equaled its majesty, and Tolkien's estate has been exceptionally assiduous in protecting his world creation.

As a result, there have been no new adventures of Bilbo, dumbed-down retellings for young-adult readers, or additional explications of events only alluded to in the master work. With the sole exception of the posthumous publication of the author's other writings (including twelve volumes of the historical background notes on the trilogy), the land of Middle-Earth has been untrodden by other writers hoping to reap from its fertile plains their own harvest of success.

But the awful truth of the matter should give these other writers pause to reconsider.

J. R. R. Tolkien did not invent Middle-Earth.

This is not to say that his works are unprotected by his copyright, or that someone else invented Bilbo and Frodo, or that other writers can be legally enjoined from continuing the Tolkien storyline.

The world of Middle-Earth, however, predates Tolkien by more than a thousand years.

True, he redecorated it, gave it a face-lift, and placed his own creations in it . . . but nonetheless Middle-Earth is no more Tolkien's sole purview than the state of New Jersey is the sole purview of David Chase, creator of HBO's *The Sopranos*.

John Ronald Reuel Tolkien was primarily an academic. After his military service during World War I, he accepted a post working on the *Oxford English Dictionary* (among his contributions were the entries *wasp* and *walrus*). In 1920 he took up a post as reader in English language at the University of Leeds, and was made a professor in 1924. In 1925 he returned to Oxford as a professor of Anglo-Saxon at Pembroke College; he retired from academia in 1959.

His scholarly projects were translations and criticism of two primal English classics—*Beowulf* and *Sir Gawain and the Green Knight*, which were originally composed in Old English/Anglo-Saxon and Middle English, respectively.

It is in *Beowulf* that Middle-Earth first makes its appearance.

Tolkien was a wonk for ancient variations of English and also one of the world's foremost experts in this area of linguistics.

In Tolkien wonk speak:

> Middle-Earth came from Midgard which was the common English transliteration of Old Norse Miðgarðr), Midjungards (Gothic), Middangeard (Old English) and Mittilagart (Old High German), from Proto-Germanic *medja-garda (*meddila-, *medjan-, projected PIE *medhyo-gharto), and as a result, is an old Germanic name for our world, the places inhabited by men, with the literal meaning "middle enclosure."
>
> In Middle English, the name became Middel-erde and resulted in the modern name Middle-earth.

Or, more simply:

Middle-Earth is another name for Midgard, which is the domain where men dwell in ancient Norse mythology—the source for the original *Beowulf* tale. It is located somewhere between the realm of the gods and the realm of the underworld (or more simply, in Judeo-Christian terms, heaven and hell).

Midgard/Middle-Earth is also the setting for *Beowulf* (mentioned specifically in the text no fewer than six times), a manuscript that Tolkien spent many hours studying and, as it turns out, being inspired by. Indeed, many archetypes and creatures that later would dwell in the pages of *The Lord of the Rings* also had antecedents in the lines of *Beowulf*.

Beowulf, like other classic works of storytelling (e.g., Homer in Greek and Virgil in Latin), purports to be history as much as invented narrative. They are all tales of a previous age in which men came to prominence and in many ways replaced the gods and other fantastic beings as the lords of this dominion.

Tolkien, as evidenced by references in his correspondence, felt the same for the setting of *The Lord of the Rings*. Indeed, Middle-Earth is only a single part of the world of Arda (Earth), and the chronological setting of his epic tale is actually many years ago in our own past, thus casting it in the same pseudo-historical mode as *The Odyssey*, *The Aeneid*, and *Beowulf*.

The lineage of the *Beowulf* story that has been passed down through countless centuries more than proves its resiliency, even if *The Lord of the Rings* has managed a greater profile on the silver screen and in the current popular media.

It is quite fair to say that no one has done a better job of embroidering this midlevel world between good and evil, gods and demons, than the old Oxford don J. R. R. Tolkien, and though he has every right to claim ownership to all of his characters and the adventures in which they partook . . . the actual world of Middle-Earth is as public a domain as the Garden of Eden, and probably a much more exciting and fertile place for adventurous storytelling to boot.

Pre-9/11 Giuliani more reviled than admired

When America was attacked by terrorists on September 11, 2001, Rudolph Giuliani rose to the occasion.

It was a Churchillian moment, when the cocky lame-duck mayor assumed the role of leader, taking command on the spot, placing himself in danger, and setting an example for the rest of the world.

At that moment he was more than a politician.

He was more than a lame-duck Republican mayor.

He was a New Yorker, and no matter what you throw at them, New Yorkers survive.

Knock a New Yorker down, and he gets right back up.

Before anyone in Washington second-guessed a plan, Giuliani was a man of action. In doing so, he earned the moniker America's mayor, and became possibly the most well-loved local politician on a national level.

Indeed, he was probably better loved on the national level than on the local level because, the awful truth of the matter is that, on September 10, he wasn't very loved at all, particularly by those who knew him best, the native New Yorkers. The city had lost sixty thousand jobs from the downturn on Wall Street, he was involved in a messy divorce, he was recovering from a bout with prostate cancer, and he was politically dying the death of the thousand self-inflicted cuts that he had engendered through his arrogance, ego, and ineptitude during his tenure as hizzoner of the Big Apple.

In Fred Siegel's book *The Prince of the City—Giuliani, New York, and the Genius of American Life*, the author starts the book's climactic chapter:

"As the new Millennium arrived, Gotham was giving birth to new industries while once dying neighborhoods were coming back to life. But for Giuliani, as a politician and a man, 2000 would prove to be the worst of years."

Siegel is overly kind.

Here are just a few of Giuliani's mistakes and failures:

- He pushed for a reform in the New York City charter as a very public vindication of his legacy, only to see it shot down in a referendum by a three-to-one popular vote against (the reform would have allowed Giuliani literally to pick his own successor should he leave office to become senator).

- He tried to evict a controversial exhibit from the Brooklyn Museum of Art because he personally found it offensive and in bad taste, spurring calls of fascistic artistic censorship.

- He came up with a plan to support an educational voucher plan for the city but undercut its tenuous support by deriding New York's public schools as "dysfunctional" and "just plain terrible," concluding, "The whole system should be blown up."

And there were, of course, many other problems.

He was divorcing his wife for a woman with whom he had been having an affair for several years, a relationship that he decided to make very public, very quickly.

Early polls had indicated that he would have lost to his Democratic opponent in the senatorial race, which would have been tantamount to humiliation in front of his Republican Party bosses.

Furthermore, he had earned nationwide notoriety for defending his police department's unnecessary fatal shooting of two unarmed and completely innocent men—Amadou Diallo and Patrick Dorismond—as well as supporting the routine rousting of young African American and Hispanic males in working-class and poor neighborhoods throughout the city on a daily basis. Using his mayoral bully pulpit for spin purposes, he placed several of the innocent victims in the position of having to "prove" their innocence while allowing the police involved the sort of privileges of counsel and consul that tipped the scales greatly in their favor.

His capriciousness of law enforcement, his cronyism, and his "do as I say or else" bullying manner had yielded numerous lawsuits and alienated many of the average New Yorkers on the street who might have supported his anti–homeless people/squeegee men/street vendor campaigns, had he bothered to follow due process and not rule by mayoral fiat (let alone the amount of money he made available for a new city-funded stadium for his beloved New York Yankees, while fiscal cutbacks were wreaking havoc on the rest of the city government).

But these and so many other sins were forgotten on September 11.

He was an inspiration for all.

How could anyone not love the guy?

And then he started talking about extending his term as mayor for the good of the city, despite legally imposed term limits, and New Yorkers were shaken back to reality.

The Rudy we knew we didn't want prior to 9/11 was back, and New Yorkers remembered why they were glad his reign was coming to an end.

Actors acting American

For the past few decades there has been a conscious effort on the part of Actors Equity to promote ethnically consistent casting in order to atone for the days when the studios would cast minority roles with Caucasian actors and actresses, resulting in such unusual performances as Boris Karloff and Sal Mineo as Indian warriors, Warner Oland and Lon Chaney as Asian gentlemen, Ricardo Montalban as a Kabuki actor, and Yul Brynner and Eli Wallach as Mexican bad men.

There was even a recent controversy concerning the movie *Memoirs of a Geisha* when non-Japanese (Chinese, Korean, etc.) Asian actors were cast as Japanese characters.

But the awful truth of the matter is that many of today's generation of thespians have become so adept at their craft that their actual ethnic/national backgrounds no longer seem to matter, and nowhere is this more evident than in the United States.

The most obvious case of this is superstar Mel Gibson, who burst onto the international scene with his performance in *Mad Max*, an Australian-made film that eventually had to be redubbed for English and American audiences due to the heavy Aussie accents of the cast. His other early roles include several appearances on Australian TV shows and major roles in such Australian films as *Tim* and Peter Weir's *Gallipoli*.

Indeed, Mel Gibson quickly became one of the most in-demand Australian actors.

But the awful truth is that Gibson has always been an American citizen. He was born in Peekskill, New York.

He didn't even move to Australia until he was twelve years old.

Mel, however, is an exception; most actors of unknown origin appear to be American-born despite their foreign fatherlands.

Anthony LaPaglia is one of the go-to guys when directors are casting a part for an Italian American, particularly if he happens to be a cop or a mobster. LaPaglia's first major part was in a TV movie as Frank Nitti, Al Capone's legendary enforcer. This was followed by other gangster roles in such films as *The Brotherhood*, *The Client*, and *Keeper of the City*, playing characters with last names such as Benedetto, Giardano, and Pesce.

Today he appears on the TV show *Without a Trace* as Jack Malone, an ethnically nondescript cop.

Unlike Mel Gibson, however, LaPaglia is from Australia, born and bred.

Another actor with a prominent TV profile, Martin Sheen, is said to have the map of Ireland on his face, something he inherited from his mother, Mary Ann Phelan. His father, however, was Spanish-born. Indeed, Sheen's full Christian name is Ramón Gerard Antonio Estévez (he changed it to Sheen in honor of a TV personality, Catholic priest Fulton Sheen).

Charlize Theron has proven herself capable of stretching as an actress with her performance as a redneck serial killer in *Monster*, as well as numerous California blond-bombshell turns in films like *Celebrity* and *The Legend of Bagger Vance* . . . but *Saturday Night Live* recently had some fun with her as she shared her lineage with Tracy Morgan as just another African American who "the man is always trying to keep down." (Theron was born near Johannesburg, South Africa.)

Still, America has always prided itself at being a melting pot.

Lest we forget—there is no more American an icon in twentieth-century entertainment history than Bob Hope, star of stage, radio, television, and screen, not to mention entertainment unit of the U.S. Armed Forces . . . and he was born in England.

The skeletons in the closet that the Academy overlooks

Every year around award season there is the persistent throng of stories relating how this or that nominee has either paid his dues with many years of consistently stellar but unheralded work, or has emerged from nowhere, debuting at the top of her profession.

But for most of these "new" stars it is a combination of both.

Because the awful truth is that many of these overnight sensations and newly discovered critical darlings have debut performances and trashy roles in their past that are more akin to skeletons in the closet than the journeyman years of craft that their PR flacks might wish you to believe.

When Sharon Stone was nominated for Best Actress for her performance in *Casino* (1995), she was already a blockbuster box-office force to be reckoned with due to her high-profile roles in *Basic Instinct*, *The Specialist*, and *Sliver*—all edgy roles in commercial films. The true width (and depth) of the canon of her work is not as succinctly encapsulated. Indeed, her cinematic past is quite checkered, including roles in such exploitation films as *Scissors* (a psycho-killer flick), *Action Jackson* (an attempt to resurrect the blaxploitation genre, with Carl Weathers on the downside of his post-*Rocky* career), *Police Academy 4*, and two Menahem Golan and Yoram Globus Allan Quatermain jungle films. Add to this such early-career made-for-TV fodder as *Calendar Girl Murders*, *The Vegas Strip War*, and *Not Just Another Affair*, and one realizes that the "overnight" in "overnight sensation" must have been an extremely long, dark, and stormy night.

Likewise, Hilary Swank, a dual Academy Award winner for her lead roles in *Boys Don't Cry* and *Million Dollar Baby* also must live with such early films on her résumé as *Buffy the Vampire Slayer* (the movie turkey, not the acclaimed TV show) and *The Next Karate Kid*, as well as paying her dues with spots on several TV series such as *Evening Shade* and *Beverly Hills 90210*.

One of Swank's Academy contemporaries, Renée Zellweger, also has a few skeletons following her. Her win as Best Supporting Actress in *Cold Mountain* as well as her nominations for *Bridget Jones's Diary* and *Chicago*, don't even hint at her early works, which include an uncredited appearance in *My Boyfriend's Back*, a comedy film about a girl whose boyfriend dies but comes back to life as a zombie because he loved her so much, or her starring role in *Texas Chainsaw Massacre: The Next Generation*.

Even triple-threat stars (critically acclaimed actor-director-producers) have their pasts.

George Clooney became an overnight success story with the debut of *ER*, a point he has acknowledged with a comment he made after being notified that NBC had picked up the series ("I think I just got my career"). Since that time Clooney has had his fair share of box-office successes, but recently he has added directing and producing to his agenda, resulting in many accolades in 2005 for his work behind the camera with *Good Night and Good Luck*, and in front of the camera in *Syriana*.

Prior to *ER*, Clooney's canon was not quite as rosy.

In addition to numerous innocuous pretty-boy roles on such television shows as *The Facts of Life, Golden Girls*, and *Roseanne,* his film work includes such less-than-distinguished titles as *Grizzly II: The Predator, Return to Horror High, Red Surf,* and *Return of the Killer Tomatoes*, the sequel to a film that is considered by many to be the worst-made horror film of all time. As the son of television news anchor Nick Clooney, and the nephew of Rosemary Clooney and José Ferrer, one might have expected a slightly less embarrassing CV.

However, even respectability and class don't preempt a skeleton or two.

Rupert Everett, the urbane, witty, and gay star of such films as *My Best Friend's Wedding* and *Dance with a Stranger* has both the unwatchable Bob Dylan starrer *Hearts of Fire* on his résumé and *Cemetery Man*, a horror film adaptation of an Italian comic book titled *Dylan Dog*.

Despite what critics say, the Bush administration did learn a lesson from the war in Iraq

Who can forget "Baghdad Bob"?

In a situation as serious and as mortally solemn as war, there is always a moment of awful absurdity that brings a dash of amusement and surreality.

Such was "Baghdad Bob"—master of the party line, Hussein's lord of the airwaves, and provocateur of broadcast firmly disconnected from the facts.

"Baghdad Bob" was Mohammed Saeed al-Sahaf (also Mohammed Said al-Sahhaf), an Iraqi diplomat and politician who came to wide prominence around the world during the 2003 invasion of Iraq, when he served as the information minister of the country.

No matter how dire the situation, "Baghdad Bob" was on the airwaves toeing the Saddam party line and encouraging the Iraqi masses to resist the foreign invaders who had no chance of winning.

In the age of the embedded reporter and twenty-four-hour-a-day you-are-there news coverage, the disconnect between Bob's broadcasts and the cameras of Fox and CNN that were embedded with the invading U.S. troops provided such unbelievable divergences from the truth as these:

March 23, 2003
BB: "The fighting is fierce and we have inflicted many damages. The stupid enemy, the Americans and the British, failed completely. They're not making any penetration."

After the U.S. forces seized control of Baghdad Airport
BB: "We butchered the force present at the airport. . . . There are no Americans there!"

April 5, 2003, as U.S. forces marched into Baghdad
BB: "Nobody came here. Those American losers, I think their repeated frequent lies are bringing them down very rapidly. . . . Baghdad is secure, is safe . . . no existence to the American troops in Baghdad at all."

After being shown pictures of the Iraqi forces surrendering
BB: "Those are not Iraqi soldiers . . . this invasion will end in failure."

Right to the bitter end "Baghdad Bob" toed the party line: Iraqi right, American wrong.

And his claims of a victorious Iraqi defense were never deterred by the mere facts that surrounded him.

On June 25, 2003, London's *Daily Mirror* reported that Bob had been captured by coalition troops at a roadblock in Baghdad. The next day al-Sahaf himself, ever the spin doctor, was interviewed by the Dubai-based al-Arabiya news channel; he said that he had turned himself in to U.S. forces. He is now believed to be living in the United Arab Emirates with his family.

Now, there have been numerous claims that the Bush administration has been overly rigid in its stay-the-course strategy in Iraq, with numerous critcs saying that the administration has not learned any lessons from their experiences on the ground.

But the awful truth of the matter is that it appears to have learned at least one lesson.

On Friday, September 2, 2005, after perhaps the largest "natural" disaster in U.S. history, when Hurricane Katrina hit the Gulf Coast and a subsequent levee breach led to the swamping of New Orleans, Michael Brown, chief of the Federal Emergency Management Agency (FEMA), held a press conference and issued statements that provided a sharp contrast to what was actually happening in devastated New Orleans—indeed, events that were being covered once again by CNN and Fox on a twenty-four-hour schedule, with correspondents on the ground and in the areas of danger where FEMA's forces had yet to tread.

At FEMA
Brown: "We learned about that [yesterday], so I have directed that we have all available resources to get that Convention Center to make sure that they have the food and water and medical care that they need."

On CNN (within an hour of the above statement)
CNN producer (at the Convention Center): "It was chaos. There was nobody there, nobody in charge. And there was nobody giving even water. The children, you should see them, they're all just in tears. There are sick people. We saw . . . people who are dying in front of you."

An evacuee (at the Convention Center): "Sir, you've got about three thousand people here in this—in the Convention Center right now. They're hungry. Don't have any food. We were told two and a half days ago to make our way to the Superdome or the Convention Center by our mayor. And which when we got here, was no one to tell us what to do, no one to direct us, no authority figure."

At FEMA
Brown: (on the issue of uncollected corpses) "That's not been reported to me, so I'm not going to comment. Until I actually get a report from my teams that say, 'We have bodies located here or there,' I'm just not going to speculate."

On CNN (previous to the above statement)
CNN producer: "We saw one body. A person is in a wheelchair and someone had pushed [her] off to the side and draped just like a blanket over this person in the wheelchair. And then there is another body next to that. There were others they were willing to show us."

At FEMA
Brown: (on the issue of the evacuation of hospitals): "I've just learned today that we . . . are in the process of completing the evacuations of the hospitals, that those are going very well."

On CNN (immediately thereafter)
CNN medical correspondent: "It's gruesome. I guess that is the best word for it. If you think about a hospital, for example, the morgue is in the basement, and the basement is completely flooded. So you can just imagine the scene down there. But when patients die in the hospital, there is no place to put them, so they're in the stairwells. It is one of the most unbelievable situations I've seen as a doctor, certainly as a journalist as well. There is no electricity. There is no water. There's over two hundred patients still here remaining."

Doctor at Charity Hospital: "We still have two hundred patients in this hospital, many of them needing care that they just can't get. The conditions are such that it's very dangerous for the patients. Just about all the patients in our services had fevers. Our toilets are overflowing. They are filled with stool and urine. And the smell, if you can imagine, is so bad, you know, many of us had gagging and some people even threw up. It's pretty rough."

At FEMA
Brown: (on reports of violence and civil unrest) "I've had no reports of unrest, if the connotation of the word unrest means that people are beginning to riot, or you know, they're banging on walls and screaming and hollering or burning tires or whatever. I've had no reports of that."

On CNN (prior and after)
CNN reporter: "From here and from talking to the police officers, they're losing control of the city. We're now standing on the roof of one of the police stations. The police officers came by and told us in very, very strong terms it wasn't safe to be out on the street."

At FEMA
Brown: (summing up) "Considering the dire circumstances that we have in New Orleans, virtually a city that has been destroyed, things are going relatively well. . . . I actually think the security is pretty darn good. There's some really bad people out there that are causing some problems, and it seems to me that every time a bad person wants to scream or cause a problem, there's somebody there with a camera to stick it in their face."

On CNN
Mayor Nagin in New Orleans: "They don't have a clue what's going on down there. . . . I continue to hear that troops are on the way, but we are still protecting the city with only fifteen hundred New Orleans police officers, an additional three hundred law enforcement personnel, two hundred fifty National Guard troops, and other military personnel who are primarily focused on evacuation."

Bystander stranded in downtown New Orleans: "They are invisible. We have no idea where they are. We hear bits and pieces that the National Guard is around, but where? We have not seen them. We have not seen FEMA officials. We have seen no one."

Crowd at the Convention Center: "We want help!"

Though one can easily acknowledge that a FEMA director should not be spending his time watching television during a national emergency, one has to question the disconnect between the information he is able to receive and the information that civilian reporters are able to broadcast from the actual site of the disaster.

Indeed, one might expect that he would be briefed on what has been on TV before he holds a press conference on TV, if for no other reason than to bring him up to date with the folks who would be watching at home.

This apparently did not happen.

There was an obvious disconnect between what you saw and what he said.

Then again, maybe there is no disconnect in FEMA's information.

We saw its presentation of the facts, the facts it wanted us to see and hear.

Maybe it is just the presentation of that information, the awful truth of the lesson learned from "Baghdad Bob": never let the facts get in the way of the party line, a lesson learned by the Bush administration.